T0096291

Derry Labour in the age of agitation, 1889–1923

Maynooth Studies in Local History

SERIES EDITOR Raymond Gillespie

This volume is one of five short books published in the Maynooth Studies in Local History series in 2016. Like their predecessors they range widely, both chronologically and geographically, over the local experience in the Irish past. Chronologically they span the worlds of 16th-century Westmeath to those of Waterford in the early 20th century. Geographically, they range across the length of the country from Derry and Antrim to Waterford and Mallow in County Cork. Socially they move from the landed and elite ecclesiastical society of Sir John Keane and Thomas Ward, dean of Connor, to the social position of children who lost their mother in 19th-century Mallow and trade unionism in Derry in the 20th century. In doing so they reveal diverse and complicated societies of the local past, and the range of possibilities open to anyone interested in studying that past. Those possibilities involve the dissection of the local experience in the complex and contested social worlds of which it is part as people strove to preserve and enhance their positions within their local societies. Such studies of local worlds over such long periods are vital for the future since they not only stretch the historical imagination but provide a longer perspective on the evolution of society in Ireland and help us to understand more fully the complex evolution of the Irish experience. These works do not simply chronicle events relating to an area within administrative or geographically determined boundaries, but open the possibility of understanding how and why particular regions had their own personality in the past. Such an exercise is clearly one of the most exciting challenges for the future and demonstrates the vitality of the study of local history in Ireland.

Like their predecessors these five short books are reconstructions of the socially diverse worlds of the poor as well as the rich, women as well as men, children as well as adults and reconstruct the way in which those who inhabited those worlds lived their daily lives, often little affected by the large themes that dominate the writing of national history. In addressing these issues, studies such as those presented in these short books, together with their predecessors, are at the forefront of Irish historical research and represent some of the most innovative and exciting work being undertaken in Irish history today. Like the other volumes in this series, they provide models that others can follow, and convey the vibrancy and excitement of the world of Irish local history today.

Maynooth Studies in Local History: Number 126

Derry Labour in the age of agitation, 1889–1923

2: Larkinism and syndicalism, 1907–23

Emmet O'Connor

FOUR COURTS PRESS

Set in 10pt on 12pt Bembo by
Carrigboy Typesetting Services for
FOUR COURTS PRESS LTD
7 Malpas Street, Dublin 8, Ireland
www.fourcourtspress.ie
and in North America for
FOUR COURTS PRESS
c/o ISBS, 920 N.E. 58th Avenue, Suite 300, Portland, OR 97213

ISBN 978–1–84682–611–5

Printed in Ireland
by eprint, Dublin.

Contents

Acknowledgments

As with volume 1, my primary debt is to the ever-obliging ladies in Derry Central Library, and the staffs of Magee College Library, the Library at Ulster University, Coleraine, and the National Library of Ireland. I am especially indebted to Ulster University for granting research leave that allowed me to complete the book. Thanks are due also to Deaglán O'Connor for help with the newspapers, Jim McBride for advice on the tramway, Séamus Breslin and Ian Miller for details on rationing, Therese Moriarty, Ed Penrose and Kevin Murphy for chasing trade union reports, Ida Milne for telling me about the flu, Nóirín Greene for comments on volume 1, Fionnuala Carlin, Terry Curran, Liam Gallagher and Daisy Mules for facilitating access to illustrations, and Ann Devenny for her photographic talent. Once again I am indebted to Professor Raymond Gillespie for commissioning the book, and agreeing that the subject deserved two volumes in this series, which has been so wonderful for local history and for young historians (like myself). None are to blame for what follows.

In February 1923, Alderman John Mark told the Londonderry branch of the Ulster Unionist Labour Association that 'if Northern Ireland lost its boundary cities of Derry and Enniskillen, they would have left a portion of country, but it would lack history'. Northern Ireland kept Derry, but Derry has lost History, which Ulster University continues to rusticate in Coleraine. It is, in the words of Cú Chulain, an insult which cannot be endured.

Volume 2 is for Talia O'Connor, who else?

Derry, 6 February 2016.

Introduction

There is a moving of men like the sea in its might;
The grand and resistless uprising of labour;
The banner it carries is justice and right,
It aims not the musket, it draws not the sabre.
But the sound of its tread over the graves of the dead
Shall startle the world and fill despots with dread,
For 'tis sworn that the land of the Fathers shall be
The home of the brave and the land of the free.

With this rhetorical flourish, Councillor James McCarron, contemporary Derry's best-known Labour leader, concluded his presidential address to the 1910 Irish Trades Union Congress (ITUC), and resumed his seat to loud cheering.[1] The verse captured the temper of the times. A landslide against the Conservatives had swept a Liberal government to power in 1906, and to head off the challenge from the nascent Labour Party it was introducing a series of industrial and social reforms, notably the Trades Disputes Act (1906), old age pensions, trade boards to enforce minimum wages in 'sweated' industries, labour exchanges, and unemployment and health insurance. Welcome as the reforms were, they failed to assuage popular discontent. The cost of living was rising, and real wages, it was believed, were falling. In fact, aggregate real wages in the United Kingdom were improving, but there were sectors and areas being left behind, and the share of wealth going to wages was falling.[2] Irish workers turned increasingly to Larkinism. The kernel of Larkinism was sympathetic action. From that root it matured into a strategy of industrial union, advocating one union for all grades, skilled and unskilled, in each industry, a politics of socialist republicanism, and a counter-culture of co-operation, sharing and solidarity. Employers resisted fiercely, and there were big disputes in Belfast (1907), Dublin (1908), Cork (1909) and Wexford (1911), on the railway (1911), and in Galway, Limerick, Sligo and Dublin (1913). The First World War generated fresh class tensions, as shortages led to hardship for wage-earners and handsome profits for farmers, employers and shopkeepers. By 1917, the government was liquidating national assets and releasing more money into the economy to keep the war effort going. With people eager to buy things unavailable in wartime, the boom rolled on into the peace. Against the backdrop of revolution in Russia, attempted revolution in Germany, Hungary and Italy, and a widespread belief that the post-war world would realize a new age of the people, 1919–20 would

be remembered in many European countries as 'the two red years'. Throughout
Europe, the surge of radicalism crashed into an economic slump and violent
political reaction in 1920.

The aim of these volumes is to examine the impact, or lack of it, at local
level, of the three waves of agitation that shaped the modern Irish Labour
movement between 1889 and 1923. Volume 1 (1889–1906) looked at the first
wave, known as new unionism, and the backwash, which became known as
old unionism. Volume 2 (1907–23) will look at Derry during the second and
third waves, Larkinism, from 1907 to 1914, and syndicalism, from 1917 to
1923. Initially, it seemed that Derry would be as much affected by Larkinism
as other cities. Local retail prices rose by 18 per cent between 1905 and 1912,
whereas wages in most categories did not change at all.[3] The building boom in
shirt-factory construction ended in 1902, the shipyard closed in 1904, and shirt
manufacturers began to cut wages in the face of increasing demand for coloured
over white shirts and competition from Germany and Austria, the sweatshops
of London's East End (from 1908), and the United States (from 1910).[4] As the
leading centre of shirt-making in the United Kingdom, Derry had thousands
of unorganized female factory workers, and one spin-off of Larkinism was the
growth of trade unionism for women. However, another consequence was Jim
Larkin's conclusion that Irish workers needed Irish unions. Derry would show
itself to be loyal to the 'amalgamateds', as cross-channel unions were called, and
become a bastion of anti-Larkinism.

Derry's economic climate began to improve in 1912, when Swan Hunter
re-opened the local shipyard. The First World War brought further prosperity
as ships and shirts were harnessed to the war effort, and the city shared in the
general upsurge of militancy from 1917. Whereas Derry was very obviously
affected by Larkin, who visited the city in 1907 and 1908, the impact of
syndicalism, like syndicalism itself, was more amorphous. Syndicalism emerged
from the perceived failure of existing versions of socialism in the 1880s. It was
distinguished by its emphasis on bringing about a revolution through trade
unions and realizing a society run by workers themselves, not professional
politicians, bureaucrats or intellectuals. Between the 1890s and its displacement
by communism after the Bolshevik revolution, it was the premier brand of
revolutionism, and captivated both Larkin and James Connolly. In Ireland
the syndicalist revival began as a reprise of Larkinite militancy in response
to wartime price inflation. Its success led to the evolution of tactics (notably
the escalation of sympathetic action into generalized action), and of strategy
(with industrial unionism giving way to the One Big Union (OBU) idea). It
also inspired the ITUC to adopt a revolutionary programme and was evident
too in efforts to build a working-class counter-culture, through co-operatives,
May Day parades, aeríochtaí in the form of social and sports days, and radical
newspapers. Syndicalism influenced most unions to a greater or lesser degree,

but was strongest in the National Union of Railwaymen (NUR) and, par excellence, the Irish Transport and General Workers' Union (ITGWU).

Volume 1 highlighted the dearth of research on Derry Labour. This is true also of the Larkinite period. The syndicalist era is a little better served, with some promising postgraduate work in progress. Derry Labour hosted one figure of historic importance when Peadar O'Donnell worked locally as an organizer for the ITGWU. The six biographies of O'Donnell skim over the Derry years, as he does himself in recollections. McCabe's 'Stormy petrel' article is more detailed.[5] The city had earlier entertained the founder of the Citizen Army, Captain Jack White, but he had lent his sword to the Irish Volunteers. Grew's work on the shirt industry ends in 1913 and the story is continued by Finlay, whose PhD thesis is particularly useful for its interrogation of recollections of O'Donnell and of shirt workers. Robinson's work is relevant for much of the 20th century, and of true value, being an MA thesis from the days when MAs were substantial contributions to knowledge.[6] The wider political backdrop is covered by Gallagher, Lacy, Murphy, and O'Brien, the economic context is superbly researched in *Atlantic gateway*, and a few passing references to Derry can be found in the expanding bibliography of union histories.[7] Of course, none of the above attempt an overview of the labour movement. Primary sources are richer. More unions in Derry meant more data in union reports, Ministry of Labour papers, and Royal Irish Constabulary (RIC) records, and the upsurge of militancy was accompanied by a stronger Labour press and greater attention to Labour in the mainstream press. The *Derry Journal* is embarrassingly ubiquitous in the endnotes, simply because it was far more informative than the *Londonderry Sentinel* or the *Derry Standard*. There is also a patchy public memory of the period, associated mainly with O'Donnell, who has a pub called after him in a street that still commemorates the defeat at Waterloo, and who was portrayed on the banner of Derry trades council. Both tributes are ironic, given his long aversion to alcohol and rejection by the trades council. Conversely, one also encounters occasional items of public history blaming O'Donnell and the trade unions for inflicting the slump on Derry.[8]

Volume 1 noted that Derry offered a choice location for studies of Labour and women and Labour and sectarianism, and a potential for challenging generalizations about Ulster made on the basis of the Belfast experience. In the 1907–23 period, it is useful too for what it says about the penetration of Larkinism, syndicalism, and the Dublin-directed ITUC in Ulster – it has been contended that their northern reach was frustrated by the stronger presence of the amalgamateds, and by the political divisions between workers – and what it tells us about the politics of Labour, links between Labour and republicanism, and Unionist mobilization against Labour.

1. Larkinism, 1907–14

Larkinism, as the employers called it to distinguish it from less militant forms of trade unionism, began in Belfast in the summer of 1907. January of that year had seen the arrival in the city of Big Jim Larkin.[1] After 15 years on the Merseyside docks, Larkin had joined a strike in 1905. His energy, courage, natural capacity for command and gift of oratory were soon recognized by James Sexton, general secretary of the National Union of Dock Labourers (NUDL), and he was appointed a full-time organizer with the union. Following good work in the north of England and Scotland, Larkin was sent to unionize the Irish ports. Ever since its bruising experiences during the height of new unionism, the NUDL had tried to apply a policy of non-militancy, and defend its members through lobbying and legal pressure to enforce fair wages contracts and health and safety legislation. But in Ireland, it faced intolerance of any form of unskilled unionism. Irish employers might accept craft unions. The craftsman was deemed to be responsible and respectable; the labourer was not, and not to be trusted with a dangerous weapon like trade unionism. In any case, the economy couldn't afford it. In the process, Larkin concluded that sympathetic action was a vital tactic for workers, and that if the Liverpool-based NUDL – known in Britain as 'the Irish union' because of the number of Irish in it at all levels – would not commit the resources to tackle Irish employer militancy, no British union would. What was needed was an Irish-based movement. It is revealing that Larkin did not begin his Irish career in Derry, though the city's dockers had, uniquely in Ireland, sustained their branch, no. 16, of the NUDL. Quietism and a peripheral location left them on the margins. Their non-militancy and loyalty to Liverpool would lead eventually to a breach with Larkin and partly explains the lack of a Larkinite revolt in the city. In many Irish cities, dockers were the only unskilled workers with effective organization after 1907, and acted as a conduit for trade unionism to the wider working class. In Derry, the dockers' differences with Larkin set local Labour at odds with the changes that were beginning to revolutionize the Irish Labour movement. But if the city did not experience a Larkinite revolt, it was not immune to Larkinism.

DERRY LABOUR IN 1907

By provincial standards, Labour in Derry was in moderately good shape before the arrival of Larkin. At a time when only Dublin, Belfast, Cork and Limerick had maintained trades councils in continuous existence – the prerequisite of any pretensions by workers to constitute a movement – and Athlone, Galway, Kilkenny, Sligo and Waterford had registered intermittent success, Derry had sustained its United Trades and Labour Council since 1888.[2] The council was vigorous in support of unionization whenever called on, and enjoyed a fair attendance of delegates at its monthly meetings in rooms at 5 Linenhall Street. Affiliated membership had fallen during the most recent downturn in the trade cycle, from 750 in 1903 to 523 in 1905, but recovered to 746 with the economic upturn in 1906.[3] The Railway Clerks' Association opened its second Irish branch in Derry in March 1906. Its long-time chairman and Gaelic Athletic stalwart, W.P. O'Doherty, would also chair the Association's Irish Divisional Council. In May, the Municipal Employees' Association, which had absorbed a local body in Belfast in 1905, formed a Derry branch with most Corporation labourers. In August, Mary Galway, secretary of the Textile Operatives' Society of Ireland, helped to launch the City of Derry Textile Operatives' Association with the support of James McCarron, and his daughter, Annie. Aside from improving conditions in Derry, Galway hoped the initiative would stop employers switching work to Derry in the event of trouble in Belfast.[4] Other unions active locally in early 1907 included the Irish National Bakers' Amalgamated Union, the Amalgamated Society of Carpenters and Joiners, the Amalgamated Union of Cabinetmakers, the Amalgamated Society of Tailors and Tailoresses (ASTT), the Postmen's Federation, the Typographical Association, the United Operative Plumbers' Association and the United Kingdom Commercial Travellers' Association.[5]

The trades council had yet to revive the May Day parades or develop a Labour party and muddled along ambiguously in politics. Ten years on, the council's president, Thomas Cassidy, would recall 'five or six Labour representatives [in Derry] but who had not really been elected as such'.[6] Two of the council's executive, James McCarron and Con Doherty, a fellow tailor, sat on the Corporation. McCarron's speeches offer a window into contemporary mentalities as they reflected the predominant outlook of the pre-Larkinite ITUC. A member of the parliamentary committee almost from its inception, McCarron was unanimously elected president of Congress, for the second time, in 1907, and a third time in 1910. On each occasion his presidential address welcomed the Liberal government's reforms, while rhetorically deploring the deficiencies in capitalism. Affable and humorous, he could reach the occasional oratorical flourish, and, as he demonstrated in the Guildhall, was passionately concerned for the welfare of children:

> Save our children in their infancy from being forced into the maelstrom of wage slavery. See to it that they are not dwarfed in body or mind or brought to a premature death by early drudgery. Give them the sunshine of the school and playground instead of the factory, the mine and the workshop (cheers). We want more schools and less jails; more books

and less arsenals; more learning and less vice; more constant work and less crime; more leisure and less greed; more justice and less revenge; in fact, more of the opportunities to cultivate our better natures – to make manhood more noble, womanhood more beautiful, and childhood more happy and bright (applause).[7]

An open admirer of the Irish Parliamentary Party, he was equally respected by pro-Union colleagues for his firm advocacy of Labour neutrality on constitutional questions. His 1907 address avoided any mention of the Irish Council bill, the government's proposal for a modest measure of devolution, and in 1910 he revealed how trenchantly he opposed Irish-based trade unionism.[8]

Derry Labour's fundamental problem was that trade unions were treading water, and scarcely effective in industrial conflict. While they had secured a measure of toleration in some instances, the standard employers' response to union demands was dismissal, and there was no shortage of blacklegs available. When 40 dockers struck over a reduction in tonnage rates for discharging the Norwegian steamer *Fredig* in May 1907, 200 men applied to take their place. Twenty were selected and gave the *Fredig* a 'flying despatch'. It was the last dock strike of this period. The NUDL hastily convened in Saint Columb's Hall and decided to generate a public sympathy campaign instead.[9] As ever, trade unionism remained weak in the city's staple industry. The annual general meeting of the Textile Operatives' Association in March 1907 drew a poor attendance. Its not certain if either of the McCarrons had a foot in the shirt factories. James was a handicraft tailor in Semple & Thompson's. His union, the ASTT, had opened a women's section in 1906 and changed its name from the Amalgamated Society of Tailors, but it continued to exclude unskilled workers, and all 100 or so members of its Derry branch were men.[10] The ASTT worried constantly about the allocation of craftwork to women, though James told a strike rally in Sligo, where this had happened, that 'If the employers were prepared to pay women the same figure as they were paying the men, then they would be prepared not only to work with them, but to admit them as members of their association'.[11] Annie gave her occupation in the 1911 census as 'nurse'. When shirt factory operatives protested about wage cuts in 1908 and 1913, employers retaliated with general lockouts to enforce the cuts. The Board of Trade recorded just 15 other strikes in the city between 1907 and 1914, involving building workers, seamen, carters and shipyardmen, and of these, five were completely unsuccessful.[12]

LARKIN IN DERRY

Larkin had been making good progress in Belfast since January 1907. By mid-February, he had recruited 400 dockers. In March a branch of the NUDL was established formally, and by April the branch had enroled 2,900 of Belfast's 3,100 dockers. Sectional strikes broke out from 26 April, and on 20 June Larkin generalized the conflict by demanding a wage increase for all cross-channel dockers. The Belfast events were soon causing tension in Derry. The RIC was sufficiently concerned to send a strike poster to Dublin Castle. Employers' posters were left alone, though the RIC reported that a local shipping agent was distributing notices offering 'good wages' to strike-breakers.[13] Whatever Derry dockers thought of their branch policy, they were keenly interested in Larkin. On Friday, 5 July, handbills were distributed advertising a meeting that evening. Larkin arrived in the city in the afternoon, and spent a few hours familiarizing himself with local conditions, though he suggested in his speech that this was not his first visit to the city. Despite the short notice, Saint Columb's Hall was packed with virtually all local dockers and carters. Shortly after 8p.m., Cassidy took the chair and introduced a man the *Derry Journal* thought 'pretty generally known'. Larkin began by outlining what had been achieved in improving wage rates in Belfast. He went on to warn of sectarianism:

> Through the efforts of the advocates of trade unionism in Belfast, they had succeeded in eliminating sectarianism and political difference from the affairs of their union and Orangeman and Catholic engaged together in one cause for their common good (Applause) … It had been said that these employers would keep the strife going until the 12th of July so as to break up the men into sections, but he knew that the workers would be alive to their own interests, and allow each to have his own idea of religion and politics without interfering with union matters (Hear, hear).[14]

Larkin knew sectarianism in Liverpool, and called himself an Ulsterman to boot, claiming to have been born in the maternal family homestead in south Down.[15] He was not so naïve as to think the problem had been disposed of in Belfast. But obviously, he thought the message relevant to Derry. Before taking questions, he concluded with a typically Larkinite appeal to manliness. 'Join the union, that is my appeal to you. If you are going to have any hope, in God's name, and in the name of humanity, be men, be free men, and join the trade union: pay your weekly contribution, and in twelve months' time, the employer will have to pay it for you (Applause)'.[16] It was a fine speech, well received, but it said nothing specific about Derry.

Events in Belfast were generating considerable interest throughout the United Kingdom, and it was hardly coincidental that drapers and their assistants met on 8 July to discuss the introduction of a summer half-holiday, and the trades council and the Textile Operatives' Association invited Mary Macarthur to Derry. Macarthur had founded the National Federation of Women Workers in 1906 after a strike in Dundee, Britain's 'juteopolis', and was one of the leading advocates of female unionization and suffrage. She spoke to shirt factory workers at a series of open-air meetings in Carlisle Square and Queen Street, with free tickets being distributed for a social. The visit culminated in a rally in the Guildhall on Friday 26 July. After the speeches, 'the labouring girlhood of the city' was entertained by a programme of Irish airs and by Professor Dan Gillen, the popular local ventriloquist, with a witty script of topical interest.[17] The Textile Operatives' Association affiliated to the Federation of Women Workers and the Women's Trade Union League, with Annie McCarron as branch secretary.[18]

Larkin returned to the city on Thursday 22 August. He was now a 'strike celebrity', having been the cause of sensational developments in Belfast, notably a police mutiny, when RIC men objected to protecting scabs and joined the strikers. Troops sent to replace the police provoked riots on the Falls Road, and killed two and wounded five others on 12 August. This time, Larkin's presence was a grander affair, and was sponsored by the trades council. The entourage included Alex Boyd, head of the Belfast Municipal Employees' Association, and Bob Morley, a popular orator on the Independent Labour Party circuit and president of the Workers' Union, one of Britain's leading general unions. It was standing room only in the Guildhall, with many squeezed onto the platform or crouching beneath it. Larkin turned up nearly half an hour late and received 'a deafening ovation'. Compared with his previous speech in Saint Columb's Hall, the oration was more radical and freewheeling, quoting Karl Marx and William Morris. At the outset, he called for 'revolution', not a bloody one, he added, but one of thought and action to transform the north of Ireland. Every reference to the fight in Belfast was 'ecstatically cheered'.[19]

On 6 September, there was a strike of local newsboys, a class of employee destined to become the mascots of Larkinism. The boys were quick to adopt Larkinism's brazen style:

> About half past eight on Monday night when Messrs Baird's van was proceeding on its circuit to distribute newspaper parcels to local agents, a rush was made at the vehicle in Foyle Street, despite the fact that a car upon which detectives were seated immediately followed the van. Some stones were thrown, one of which broke a glass panel in the rear of the van.

Efforts by the RIC to arrest the newsboys led to a riot in Guildhall Square.[20] The strike was one of many efforts at unionization inspired by Larkin. The National Federation of Women Workers scored partial successes in resisting wage cuts at Tillie & Henderson's and Leinster Brothers. Despite filling Carlisle Square with a protest meeting, the trades council was unable to persuade William Tillie to talk to the union. Playing the Orange card, Tillie placed outsize advertisements in the 'wanted' columns of the *Derry Standard* and the *Londonderry Sentinel* seeking '20 good shirt makers, constant employment and highest wages. Apply

(*Above*) Shirt cutters. 2. (*Below*) Shirt factory operatives. Note the difference in working conditions.

immediately before the machines are filled up'. The advertisements were still running when the dispute ended after four weeks, with the workers accepting a reduced pay cut.[21] Leinster Brothers locked out their girls even closer to Christmas, and again trades council affiliates responded swiftly with pledges of financial aid and secured an 'amicable' settlement through mayoral arbitration. The Federation of Women Workers celebrated with a rally in the Guildhall. Days later the Workers' Union and the Municipal Employees' Association also held organization rallies in the city hall.[22] Most remarkably, the trades council unanimously endorsed James McCarron's proposal that it form a branch of the Social Democratic Federation, the leading British Marxist party. McCarron insisted at length that socialism was not against religion and argued that wealth should not be just for those who could 'loll about in carriages and motors [and] perhaps sooner or later, aerial machines (laughter)'. Winding up the debate, the council chairman, Robert Wilson, JP, said he 'had long been a socialist ... Sound socialism, when rightly practiced, was only practical Christianity'.[23] One measure of Larkin's importance is the decline of Labour agitation in Derry in 1908, when Big Jim shifted his attention from the north to Dublin and Cork. A branch of the Amalgamated Society of Railway Servants was established in May, but otherwise it was a depressing year, noted for the refusal of the Corporation to increase municipal labourers' rates from a miserly 15s. per week to 17s., and a five-day lockout of over 1,000 shirt workers in September to enforce a pay cut. The lockout was precipitated by a strike in one department, again suggesting that employers had to deal with an element of solidarity and cohesion among workers, despite their lack of a union.[24]

DERRY'S BREAK WITH LARKIN

Larkin's relations with Sexton deteriorated steadily in 1908, partly on policy and partly on personality grounds. Belfast made Sexton more determined than ever to curb militancy. Conversely, it led Larkin to conclude that the only way to beat the employers was by extending struggle through sympathetic action. Also, Larkin was getting very popular with Irish workers, and the more popular he became, the more insubordinate he became. The tipping point was reached in Derry, on a routine inspection, in late November. Ignoring orders to move on to Aberdeen, Larkin entrained for Dublin to take command of emerging strike movements. Sexton warned him on 28 November that the union executive had strongly condemned him for 'acting contrary to instructions', and empowered the general secretary to suspend him. On 7 December, Sexton wrote the letter of suspension.[25] With no income and little alternative, Larkin took the most fateful step in the history of Irish Labour and called a meeting of what was styled 'the Irish executive' of the NUDL. No such body existed, and Larkin may have simply summoned a few picked men. 'Delegates' from Belfast, Cork,

Dublin, Dundalk and Waterford attended, suggesting that Larkin had no ally in the other two branches, Derry and Drogheda. The 'executive' met on 28 December 1908 in Dublin, and agreed to found the ITGWU.[26]

Larkin's immediate concern was to carry the NUDL's Irish branches into the ITGWU. In Dublin, he spoke of the union as an Irish departure, whereas in the north he played down its nationalist rationale, challenging Sexton to resign and let them both contest an election for general secretary.[27] Sexton would probably have let Ireland go. He was a sensitive man, and pained that his running fight with Larkin was damaging his reputation in the Labour movement. He was afraid too that Larkin might make a bid for his job, or form a rival union in Britain. Support for Larkin and antagonism to Sexton led Clydeside, Dundee, and Bo'ness dockers to break away from the NUDL and launch the Scottish Union of Dock Labourers in 1911.[28] However, Boyd, Larkin's deputy in the Belfast dock strike and a loyalist, did not want to see Belfast workers switching from a British to an Irish union. Leaving the (Catholic) deep-sea dockers to the ITGWU, Boyd called on Sexton to rally the (Protestant) cross-channel men to the NUDL.[29] Both Boyd and Sexton were joined in Belfast by William J. McNulty from the Longtower, veteran secretary of the Derry dockers and carters. Next day, Sexton arrived in the NUDL rooms at Orchard Street to persuade Derry to stick with 'the old union'. Making it a matter of policy rather than personality, a choice between the NUDL and moderation or the ITGWU and strikes, McNulty told his members: 'he deprecated strikes … He never yet knew of a strike which benefited the worker', and urged the election of Labour MPs instead. Whether the dockers made up their minds on the basis of policy or personality is debatable. As the chairman of the branch suggested, the men's respect for McNulty was crucial to their decision to stay with the NUDL. The meeting declared:

> our adhesion to the union, and strongly condemn the action of the late organiser and other branch officials of Belfast in their attempt to create a division in the ranks of the union by the formation of an opposition organization, and request the general secretary to exercise the power vested in him to take the necessary legal steps to secure the property of the union.[30]

On 15 January, the NUDL started court action to repossess union books and offices in Belfast from the ITGWU. No effort was made to recover union property south of the Boyne.[31] Another partition was underway.

The dispute then came before the ITUC as the ITGWU asked the parliamentary committee to stop the NUDL blacklegging in Belfast – its Belfast branch was colluding with employers to prevent work going to ITGWU men – and Sexton rejoined with a request to have the ITGWU debarred from Congress as a breakaway. When the annual Congress met in Limerick in May, Sexton was present with two Derrymen, McNulty and T. O'Hara, and a Drogheda delegate. Coincidentally, Cassidy was there too, to defend his union, the British-based Typographical Association, in a dispute with the Dublin Typographical Provident Society. A recommendation from the Congress's standing orders committee that the ITGWU be admitted met fierce opposition from amalgamateds. Fearing it would generate a snowball of pressure for Irish-based trade unionism, delegates from Ulster in particular raised the prospect of a split between Irish and British unions. McCarron went so far as to say it might mean 'the wiping out of [the parliamentary] Committee and trade unionism'. On his feet in the gallery, Larkin roared 'traitor, skunk, betrayer, tools of England'. It was agreed to refer the dispute to a seven-man investigation committee, one of whom was Hugh McCallion, Derry NUDL.[32] Diplomatically, the committee found that there was 'no real justification' for the ITGWU's secession from the NUDL and, equally, that the ITGWU was a bona fide union, entitled to recognition.[33] The findings still had to be endorsed by the next annual Congress, in Dundalk in May 1910. Leading off for the old guard, E.W. Stewart argued that admission of the ITGWU should be postponed pending the resolution of its dispute with the NUDL over 'the ownership of a large sum of money'. McNulty went further and moved an amendment to the committee's report, deleting the reference to the ITGWU's bona fide status.[34] Fortunately for Larkin, attitudes in Congress had softened since 1909. Possibly because of the ITGWU's lacklustre performance on the industrial front, there was less anxiety about its implications for the amalgamateds. To 'loud cheers', McNulty's amendment was defeated by 38 to 22 votes. Another amendment, for the affiliation of the ITGWU, was carried 42 to 10. It was a bitter moment for McCarron, who was serving his third term as Congress president. His decision that the matter would have to be ratified by the parliamentary committee after lunch provoked Larkin into storming from the gallery to the floor, and speaking 'in a very excited manner', denouncing some of the delegates as 'notorious blacklegs' and enemies of trade unionism. After interventions had exposed his ruling as petty, McCarron was embarrassed into admitting Larkin and the five ITGWU delegates immediately. Larkin too relented, apologizing for his remarks. It was still too much for McCarron, who withdrew his name from the elections to the parliamentary committee, in which he had topped the poll in 1909, and announced that he was severing his connection with Congress. He attributed the decision not to Larkin, but to the election to the parliamentary committee of P.T. Daly, an old Fenian and Larkinite, who had once refused to meet a minister of the crown. It was a sour end to a distinguished career.[35]

Nor did the recrimination end there. McCarron, Stewart and two officers of the Workers' Union threatened libel actions over Larkin's report of the Congress in James Connolly's monthly, the *Harp*. On McCarron, the report claimed that Patrick Thompson, his employer and then mayor of Derry, had tried to prevent Larkin speaking in the city in 1907, and implied that McCarron was an 'uncle Tom', unwilling to challenge Thompson, and tolerated by employers because he was such a woeful organizer.[36] The libel threats destroyed hopes of transferring the paper permanently from New York to Dublin, and the June issue was the last.[37] McCarron continued to attend the annual Congresses as a delegate, and he and McNulty remained a thorn in Larkin's side. At the famous Clonmel Congress in 1912, which, notionally, established the Labour Party, Larkin proposed that 'a closer union should exist between the various trades and labour bodies in Ireland' and to this end the parliamentary committee be instructed to draw up a constitution for 'an Irish Federation of Trades'. It was, he said, 'true industrial unionism. The body he spoke of should be the one to rule trade unionism in Ireland'. As 'one big union' would entail the end of British unions in Ireland, McCarron and McNulty led the opposition. 'The employers were organized in a world-wide organization (hear, hear), and Mr Larkin now wanted the workers to confine themselves to Ireland alone', said McCarron. 'If this resolution was passed his Society or any other amalgamated Society would not send their delegates to any future Irish Trades Congress (hear, hear)'. The scheme was rejected by 29–23 votes. The amalgamateds still had a majority in Congress. Larkin had better luck in the hustings for the parliamentary committee, and was elected chairman of a committee, which was almost entirely Larkinite. His buoyancy at the close of proceedings was reflected in his proposal that the 1913 Congress assemble in Cork, the scene of a humiliating defeat of the ITGWU in 1909. He struck a defiant note: 'He, personally, would be very glad to renew acquaintance with the men of Cork. They had been beaten there once, but they could not expect to win every time, and they would win there again (hear, hear)'.[38]

Larkin proved to be an awkward chairman of the parliamentary committee. His personality problems were worsening as interminable assaults on his character from employers and Labour critics took their toll. On 22 March 1913 one of his lieutenants, William O'Brien, sent a gloomy post to Connolly:

> Things are in a very bad way still … We hear that there is to be a big fight put up against us in Cork. We are told that a record number of delegates will attend from Cork City, and that there is to be a whip up of all the 'old gang' from all parts of the country. [D.R.] Campbell, Daly, Larkin, and myself are at all cost to be removed from the PC [Parliamentary Committee]. McCarron, I have reason to believe, will be one of the big guns against us. He was a member of the PC from its inception to 1910, and up to that year always came out on top.[39]

Travelling south on the train to Cork, endlessly relighting his pipe, Larkin fretted about the residue of animosity among local trade unionists and talk of how he'd be 'kicked through the streets'.[40] He, Connolly and McCarron clashed repeatedly during the Congress debates, over Irish-based trade unionism and an Irish Labour Party. Expressing their resentment as the sun went down on the old Redmondites who had managed the pre-Larkinite ITUC:

He (McCarron) held that they should put their case before the Irish Party, who represented all sections in Ireland, and should not go behind their backs to an English Party. The time was inopportune for the formation of an Independent Labour Party in Ireland, but that was what Mr Larkin apparently wanted. His own ideal was a cosmopolitan labour movement, but for the present he placed the Home Rule question first as regards Ireland, and he did not see why the deputation who went across to England should go to the English Labour Party in connection with that question while they had the Irish Party.[41]

Surprisingly, the proceedings went well for Larkin. The 'old gang' fared badly in the elections for the parliamentary committee, and it seemed that the ITUC was more Larkinite than ever. McNulty topped the list of 'also rans', and when he sarcastically congratulated the delegates on choosing a 'scab' parliamentary committee, he was unanimously expelled from the Congress, at Connolly's request.[42]

1913

In June 1911, there was a sudden outbreak of strikes in Britain, and what became known as 'the great labour unrest' rolled on until the World War. When stoppages of seamen and railwaymen extended to Ireland, Larkin responded, calling for sympathetic action. As his confidence grew, his union took up workers' grievances wherever it found them. By mid-1913, many employers were willing to recognize the ITGWU in return for one month's notice of strikes, an arbitration scheme, and some restriction of sympathetic action, much to the disdain of nationalist Ireland's puissant capitalist, William Martin Murphy. Murphy insisted that business could not survive what he called 'the system of syndicalism, or sympathetic strikes', and compared Larkin with Emile 'King' Pataud, the syndicalist leader of French electricians, who was famous for spectacular industrial action, and had been run out of France.[43] Murphy was determined to do the same to Larkin. He got his chance when Larkin tried to organize his employees on the Dublin trams and in Independent Newspapers, and rallied 404 fellow employers to smash the ITGWU.

Derry was relatively quiet during 'the great labour unrest'. There were no strikes in 1910, and it is doubtful if anyone noticed Connolly returning from America via Moville on the Anchor line's *Furnissia* on Monday 25 July. Next morning he telegrammed from Derry: 'Just landed. Arrive Dublin Tuesday', and caught an early train, steaming into the Great Northern terminus at Amiens Street, Dublin, at 1p.m. He was anxious to have his first meeting with Larkin, who was due in court on the Wednesday, and likely to start a prison sentence the same day.[44] In November he wrote to his family in America, promising 'second-class tickets to Londonderry', and welcomed them to Derry in early December.

His daughter Nora recalled that they stayed overnight in a hotel, everything seeming 'strange and small' to the returned Yanks, and her father took them on a tour of the walls and told them the story of the siege.[45] Some minor incidents occurred in 1911 as the great shipping and rail disputes brushed the city with their wingtips. The Amalgamated Society of Railway Servants in Dublin joined a British national strike on the morning of 18 August, and by afternoon the stoppage had spread to 30 men in the goods yard of the Great Northern at Foyle Road. The national strike ended in victory on 21 August. Trouble on the railway rumbled on. In September, the Railway Clerks' Association hosted a meeting of numerous unions in protest at the dismissal of a colleague on the Londonderry and Lough Swilly Railway.[46] An acid test came on 20 September, when the Amalgamated Society of Railway Servants called a national sympathetic strike for the reinstatement of two porters at Dublin's Kingsbridge station, dismissed for refusing to handle what Larkin called 'tainted goods', i.e., goods coming from or going to a company in dispute. It was the most important strike in Ireland between 1907 and 1913. To employers, it was Larkinism on the railway. A large meeting of the Derry Merchants and General Employers' Association promised the railway companies every assistance and urged the lord lieutenant to provide adequate police and troops to guarantee loading and delivery. Derry railwaymen, like most others in Ulster, did not join the strike.[47] When it collapsed on 4 October, railway militancy had been severely checked. Two small strikes followed in 1912, and there were seven disputes in 1913, of which two were significant in size and duration. In February, 1,200 shirt and collar workers were idle, out for three weeks to enforce a wage cut. As in 1908, a strike in one department was met with a general lockout. In August 200 building craftsmen struck for three months to win a pay rise.[48]

The great Dublin lockout was well reported in the local press. The *Derry Standard* was the most hostile to Labour, with the *Londonderry Sentinel* not far behind. Unionists regarded Labour militancy as a threat to society and to the constitution. Nationalists were ambiguous. The *Derry Journal* gave more space to Labour affairs and blamed the authorities for the riots in Belfast in 1907, but turned anti-Larkinite during the lockout, and revealed its acceptance of the employers' perspective in heading its coverage 'Syndicalism'. Nationalists took an added interest in the lockout following the appointment of a public enquiry into disturbances in Dublin, and went to court in pursuit of a similar enquiry into 'Orange hooliganism' after the Apprentice Boys' parade on 12 August; violence the Unionist press attributed to 'nationalist ruffianism'.[49] All three Derry papers could agree on their antipathy to Larkinism. An editorial in the *Sentinel* on 23 September noted with satisfaction:

> A feature of the situation has been the failure of Mr Larkin to obtain a foothold either in Belfast or Londonderry. Belfast got enough of the gentleman on the occasion of the last strikes there. As for Londonderry, its

dock workers, carters &c, were warned in time against Larkinite methods, with the result that the last visit which the would-be dictator paid to the city on a notable occasion was of short duration, and bore no fruit from his point of view.

The NUDL did indeed twist the knife. In one instance, a cargo of Guinness, blacked by ITGWU men in Sligo, was diverted to Derry.[50] Outraged by police attacks on workers at the start of the lockout, Sexton supported Larkin initially. By November, British Labour leaders were changing their tune, as Larkin identified with the 'rebels' of the British trade union rank-and-file, and pilloried their leaders for not approving sympathetic action to beat William 'Murder' Murphy. On 25 November, James O'Connor Kessack denounced the ITGWU at a meeting of Derry dockers and carters. Kessack, a Scot, had succeeded to Larkin's job in the NUDL and was on an organizing tour of Ireland. Unusually for a NUDL official dealing with a very clannish class of men, he had never been a docker, and owed everything to Sexton. He and Larkin had clashed before, and Larkin had accused him of sending scabs to Dublin. 'Larkin', said Kessack, 'was not only a fool but a knave ... The greatest obstacle to the uplifting of the working classes ... was Larkin and men like him ... workers ... should never let themselves be cut adrift from their fellow-workers across the Channel'.[51]

Were the dockers better off for following Sexton's strategy of seeking to improve working conditions by invoking the law or putting political pressure on employers rather than strikes? Exceptionally, the port of Derry was never de-casualized. On the other hand, many dockers liked the freedom that went with casualism, and feared that registration would be used to monitor the workforce. Jim's brother, Pete, led Liverpool dockers against it, saying it would be used to blacklist militants. When Sexton got an agreement to replace casualism with a registration scheme in 1911, Jim denounced him in the *Irish Worker*.[52] The Derry branch would hardly have flourished without delivering for its members, and in 1912 it had a membership of 400 and Kessack thought it in good shape. A court case in 1913 suggests it had enforced an unofficial closed shop to the extent that 'button men' were given priority in employment, and a man seeking preference without the union button would be reminded that accidents happen easily on the waterfront. The union also controlled the manning and allocation of men to tonnage squads.[53] At the same time, the revitalization of Labour in Derry owed much to Larkin's inspiring crusade. Thanks to Larkinism and the 'great labour unrest', the NUDL changed its name to the NUDL and Riverside Workers, and amended Sexton's 'dockers only' policy to widen membership to carters and all unskilled operatives, including shirt factory girls. Through the carters it was involved in the most dramatic Derry strike of this period. On 4 February 1914, 140 men of the carters' section struck seven companies in pursuit of an increase in wages from 18s. to 22s. per week and a 55-hour week. Next day, there were 'stirring scenes' as pickets stopped strike-breaking waggons and lorries. Twenty extra police were drafted in from Coleraine, and five mounted constables patrolled the streets. Kessack negotiated a settlement on 9 February when the Derry Merchants' and General Employers' Protection Association offered 20s. for a 56½ hour week. Dockers too adopted a more militant approach and secured pay increases in April, and the NUDL made a fresh attempt to organize shirt factory workers, bringing Ester Young from London to explain the Trade Boards Act.[54]

On the eve of the First World War, Labour in Derry was in better shape than ever. The introduction of minimum rates for shirt factory workers under the Trade Boards Act (1909) promised to consolidate the tenuous presence of trade unionism in the staple industry. The ITUC had lobbied hard and successfully for the inclusion of Ireland in the Act, with McCarron pressing the case for clothing workers.[55] Trade unionism itself was changing as the 'great labour unrest' prompted a quest for 'greater unionism' through a merger mania and an ambition to recruit all grades. Women in Derry could join the ASTT from 1913, when it opened its books to factory operatives. Its Londonderry Factory Workers' branch had 100 members in 1914.[56] In 1912, Swan Hunter re-launched the Derry shipyard as the North of Ireland Shipbuilding Company, bringing jobs in traditionally militant occupations. The yard's labour force rose from 320 men in January 1913 to 750 by December.[57] As Serb assassins prepared for Sarajevo in June 1914, the Chamber of Commerce met in the Guildhall to form an artisans' dwellings company. Estimating that at least 300 houses would be needed to accommodate expanding demands from the shipyard, the Chamber emphasized that balance of yin and yang which Belfast had achieved and which, maddeningly, had eluded Derry: 'Without proper housing accommodation they could not, therefore, expect the shipyard to extend, and unless they had male employment they would also be unable to supply the steadily increasing demand for female labour in the shirt trade'.[58] In other sectors, craft unions were holding their own, and general unionism was expanding. Reflecting the buoyancy, the trades council was hale and hearty, and the 'old guard' could claim some vindication from Larkin's defeat in the lockout and departure for the United States in October 1914. Derrymen were still smarting from Big Jim. 'He was an impartial chairman', Cassidy quipped at the 1914 Congress, 'He had no respect for what delegate he sat upon'.[59] After McCarron declined appeals at the Congress to run for the executive to ensure it contained a Derry voice, Cassidy manned the gap, and would remain involved with the ITUC leadership until 1936. McNulty too contested the executive in 1914 and suffered a humiliating defeat.[60] He had the consolation of becoming the senior NUDL official in Ireland when Kessack enlisted in the wartime army, and the satisfaction of poaching a port from the ITGWU in 1915. Connolly had negotiated a wage increase for Waterford dockers, which fell short of expectations. When he refused to sanction strike action, they called him a 'master's man'. Storming out of the hall, he told them to get another official. They got McNulty.[61]

2. Boom, 1914–20

For workers on the home front between 1914 and 1918, it was a war of two halves. The first half stored up class tensions over food shortages, rising prices and profiteering by employers, shopkeepers and farmers as those on fixed incomes saw their real wages dwindling. On Britain's entry into the war, the British Labour Party, trade unions, trades councils and co-operative societies established the War Emergency Workers' National Committee to influence public policy. That this was to be an alternative to militancy was made plain by the party and unions on 24 August 1914 when they urged an end to all strikes for the duration.[1] Committees on Production evolved on an ad hoc basis to fix wage rates, improve output and manage labour supply, and while trade unionism extended and wages rose in tandem with state regulation, the government was slower to control prices. A Food Controller was appointed in December 1916, and price control phased in on a local and selective basis at the discretion of his officials. Rationing of petrol was introduced in 1916, and food rationing in 1918. As concern mounted, Westminster appointed the Sumner committee, which estimated that between July 1914 and July 1918 the cost of living for working-class families in Britain rose by an estimated 74 per cent, with the burden falling most heavily on the families of unskilled workers, whose costs increased by 81 per cent compared with 67 per cent for the families of skilled men.[2] In Belfast, trade unions, co-operative societies, and women took to the streets in hunger marches. The ITUC convened its first special congress in December 1916 to discuss what was called the food supply crisis. The Congress executive then met the chief secretary for Ireland to request statutory maximum prices for bread and coal, depots for the supply of coal and milk, and an embargo on potato exports.[3] Derry's agonies were exacerbated by the decline in civilian demand for ships and shirts and the authorities' tardiness in mobilizing these obviously war-related industries. The escalation of the U-boat campaign from 1916 prompted a shift in government policy.

The level of protest in Britain, underpinned by growing production needs and the ever-increasing manpower shortage, alarmed the government into a major relaxation of wage restraint in 1916, and a liquidation of state assets to release more money into the economy to keep the war effort going. From 1916 to 1920, wages grew faster than prices, overtaking pre-war real levels by 1919–20. In the nature of capitalism, the money was there only for those who could get it. If more and more occupations were coming under state regulation, employers quibbled about the meaning and application of wage awards, and as the labour shortage was less acute in Ireland than cross-channel, they were in a position to do so. Bargaining power depended on two things: importance to the war economy, and collective organization. Ships and shirts made Derry well-placed in the first respect, after the teething troubles at least. A surge in trade union membership provided the second condition. Membership of the ITUC jumped from under 100,000 in 1916 to 229,000 in 1920, when there were probably another 30,000 trade unionists in Ulster not affiliated to Congress for political reasons.[4] Labour was by now identified with the independence movement, and industrial relations too were affected by revolution at home and abroad, and the expectation that the post-war world would realize a new age of the people. Peace brought even greater prosperity, with the release of pent-up consumer demand, and by January 1920 over 5,000 had been drawn to the city in search of employment.[5] The *annus mirabilis* of the 'long' 1919 rolled on until the summer of 1920, when it seemed that Labour would get stronger and stronger and life would get better and better.

WAR

It was a semi-detached war for Ireland, not total in the way 1939–45 would be, even for neutral Éire. In much of life and politics, the focus stayed elsewhere, oblivious to the slaughter grinding on relentlessly. Captain Jack White, co-founder of the Citizen Army and sometime Tolstoyan anarchist, moved to Derry in May 1914 to train the Irish Volunteers. Looking out on the city from McMahon's Hotel on the East Wall, he described the marching and counter-marching by the Volunteers and the Ulster Volunteer Force as 'a powder mine'.[6] Jostling for Britain's favour, Unionists and Nationalists rivalled each other in urging support for the war, but the passions would not be parked by the trouble in Europe. The Catholic clergy and the *Derry Journal* switched allegiance to Sinn Féin after John Redmond's acceptance of temporary partition in July 1916. The city's first Sinn Féin cumann, the P.H. Pearse, was formed in August 1916. Weeks later, 2,500 attended a Sinn Féin meeting in Saint Columb's Hall.[7] The Redmondites were trounced in the 1918 general election, Eoin MacNeill (Sinn Féin) winning 7,335 votes to 7,020 for Sir Robert Anderson (Unionist) and 120 for William Davey (Nationalist).

Equally, all aspects of life in Derry were touched by the war, directly in some ways. Belgian refugees arrived in 1914. Britain's grand fleet anchored in Lough Swilly in October 1914, and Buncrana boomed with the construction of naval fortifications. U-boats could determine the goods in shops from 1916. French Department of Agriculture officials toured the west and north-west in 1918 seeking labourers for the French harvest.[8] An estimated 4,000 enlisted locally in the forces, and 756 men and one woman, a nurse, were recorded as the city's war dead.[9] The *Derry Journal* continued to give the western front substantial and pro-British coverage, and featured outsize recruitment ads almost to the armistice. The great, germane question is why men joined up. The reasons may vary from patriotism through the political calculation of Redmond and Edward Carson, to boredom or a sense of adventure. One neglected factor is class. A disproportionately high number of recruits were unskilled urban labourers, the sector most badly hit by profiteering and the dislocation of employment during the first half of the war. With rural labour in greater demand from the outset, agricultural workers were less likely to enlist. For unemployed or unskilled men with families, army pay was very good. An infantry private earned 1s. a day, all found, and perquisites normally raised this to 1s. 9d. If married, he had an allotment deducted, and in return his wife received a separation allowance, which varied with the number of children under 16 years. Unlike the basic pay, the separation allowances were increased regularly. A recruit in September 1914, with a wife and two children, could expect 12s. 3d. weekly for himself, less an allotment of 3s. 6d. His wife would receive 17s. 6d., giving the family a gross income of 26s. 3d. per week. Of recruits in Ireland, about 70–80 per cent of the ranks in 'Kitchener's army', the volunteers of 1914–15 whose first big push was at the Somme, had been unskilled workers, at a time when the sector comprised 28 per cent of men between 20 and 45 years. Around 30 per cent of the ranks were illiterate.[10] Those who survived often faced the need to seek fresh employment. One tonnage docker, Archibald Ball from Howard Street, a veteran of the Boer War, rejoined the army in 1916, impressed by a placard in the office of Samuel Morrison and Co., coal merchant, promising recruits their jobs back on demobilization. When Morrison's refused to take him on, and the NUDL declined to make room for him in a tonnage squad, he sued the company for £50. The case revealed a little of working practices and class prejudice.

> Ball: If the defendants had no boat, he could take up employment elsewhere. The Dockers' Union specified that a certain squad could be employed at a boat.
> His Honour: Do you call that free labour, because I don't.
> Counsel for Morrison: That is one of the difficulties the masters have to contend with.
> His Honour: Yes, and it is destroying the country, and the labourers are the first that will suffer.
> Counsel for Ball: If men like this had not gone to the war what would have happened the country?
> His Honour: Probably there would have been better men to go. There is very little credit in that.
> Counsel for Ball: Very little credit for a labourer who went to the war?
> His Honour: Yes …[11]

The case was dismissed. Nationalists boycotted the 'peace day' celebrations that followed the Treaty of Versailles, and a local branch of the Irish Nationalist Veterans' Association was formed in August 1919.[12]

At home, the abiding problems were rising prices and shortages. As early as February 1915 the Inishowen Poor Law Guardians were calling on the government to 'put an end to the heartless ring of monopolists who fatten on the misery and oppression of the poor'.[13] Profiteering in coal led the Corporation to charter colliers and create a municipal supply in 1916.[14] The Chamber of Commerce noted the repeated dearth of two of the most essential foodstuffs, flour and sugar, over 1917–18.[15] There were criticisms too of the application of control orders. Control extended to the price of livestock and was often seen in Ireland as a means of penalizing Irish farmers and meat processors to satisfy British consumers. 'Food controlling in this country has created many anomalies and led to a state of lamentable confusion', complained the *Derry Journal*.[16] Moreover, many wartime restrictions would continue until 1920–1. As employment prospects improved, housing joined the list of shortages with the influx of migrants looking for work. Lured all the way from Waterford were the parents of Dr Noel Browne. Mother and child were miserable in a paraffin-lit hovel in the Bogside. Noel recalled his parents packing 'blindingly white starched' collars for a pittance as black rats scurried around the yard.[17] The cost of digs was a major issue in the shop assistants' strike of 1918.[18] After war, death and near famine, came pestilence. The epidemic influenza of 1918–19 infected 27,320 people in the city and county, almost 20 per cent of the population, and claimed the lives of 683.[19]

TRADE UNIONS AND THE WAGES MOVEMENT

The war transformed industrial relations, though the changes came mainly after the armistice; it now became necessary to contain militancy and smooth the transition to peace-time production. A Ministry of Labour was carved out of the Board of Trade in 1916, and it opened an Irish department in 1919. The Trade Boards Act (1918) allowed the Ministry to enforce minimum rates, set up the industrial court, and pave the way for the introduction of 15 new trade boards in 1919–20. Those of particular relevance to Derry covered boot and shoe repair, aerated waters, tailoring, dressmaking, millinery, laundering, tailoring, milk distribution, flax and waste reclamation.[20]

Following the introduction of the Trade Boards Act (1909), employers came together in the Londonderry Shirt and Collar Manufacturers' Association in 1913. When the shirtmaking trade board proposed 3½d. per hour for a 50-hour week for women in June 1914, the Manufacturers' Association pleaded for a reduction of Irish rates to offset transport costs. The board upheld the appeal in 1915, and the differential with Britain became a chronic grievance. Coincidentally, the financial impact of the war was reversed. In April the Board of Trade's *Labour Gazette* noted that employment in the industry in Derry had fallen over the past year and 23 per cent of workers were on short time. On

26 May, the *Derry Journal* reported that 'at last' the city's shirt factories were getting government contracts. Membership of the ASTT's Londonderry (Factory Workers) branch rose to 500 members in 1915 and 3,354 in 1917. Jealous of their status as the male elite of the trade, the Londonderry Shirt, Collar and Underclothing Cutters' followed a separate line and merged with the Shirt and Collar Cutters' Union of Ireland in 1915. Cutters struck in November 1915 for the removal of a forewoman, and when M'Intyre, Hogg, Marsh & Co. introduced two women into their cutting room in March 1916, arguing that the company needed to prepare for conscription, the union persuaded them to leave, offering two months wages in compensation. The firm re-employed them, pushing the union into another unsuccessful strike. It was an exceptional incident. Dilution, which helped to create the Scottish shopstewards movement and 'Red Clydeside', did not become an issue in Ireland. In 1919, the Shirt and Collar Cutters' Union, with some 280 members in Derry, joined the British-based United Garment Workers' Union (UGW).[21]

The North of Ireland Shipbuilding Company remained on a pre-war production footing initially and employment at the yard dwindled to 200 as the government prioritized naval construction and directed men and materials to Clydeside and Tyneside. Its fortunes changed in 1916, when priority was given to replacing merchantmen lost to the U-boats. Four new slipways were built, together with houses and hostels to accommodate a workforce swollen to over 2,000. In May 1918, the Shipyard Male Voice Choir gave its first public performance to a 'large and enthusiastic audience' in the Guildhall. The yard also produced a soccer club, and in May 1920 the company sponsored a carnival of athletics, trotting and driving at the Brandywell. Since 1912, the National Amalgamated Union of Labour (NAUL), which had organized semi-skilled shipyardmen in Belfast from the 1890s, and, like Swan Hunter, was Tyneside-based, had recruited in the Derry yard and it was joined by craft unions.[22] Craft and grade distinctions made British shipbuilding notoriously prone to disputes over demarcation and differentials, and operating in more stressed and volatile times, North of Ireland Shipbuilding had many more industrial disputes than its predecessors. Trevisa Clarke, managing director of the yard, who had a gift for antagonizing business colleagues and the Corporation as much as workers, took a tough line against militancy in 1919, prosecuting striking apprentices for breach of contract under the Employer and Workmen Act (1875) and threatening to close the company.[23] Clarke ensured that wages in Derry were lower than in the Belfast yards, where rates for unskilled men were well below cross-channel levels. The introduction of trade boards after the war narrowed the gap, much to Clarke's irritation.[24]

The NAUL became active too in the city's third main industry, distilling.[25] Distillerymen had their own war-related difficulties and held a mass meeting in the Dockers' Hall in Orchard Street in May 1915 to protest against the Chancellor's proposals to restrict the liquor trade.[26] War, and the consolidating

3. Harvesting at
Gransha, *c.*1930,
when agriculture
was still relatively
labour intensive.

voice of women, generated a substantial push for the prohibition of alcohol. If, before the war, the continuing support for the NUDL did most to distinguish Derry from southern Labour, the NAUL was emblematic of the divergence of north and south after 1914, as it became the general union for Ulster, recruiting sectors which joined the ITGWU in the south, and organizing on the land and in small towns like Dungiven.[27] By mid-1917, Derry's no. 112 branch had sections for distillery workers, bacon curers, gasworkers, bleach workers, labourers and warehousemen.[28] In 1919, the NAUL had three branches in the city, for the shipyard, the factories and general workers.[29] The RIC commented on progress in Donegal, where NAUL branches were flourishing in Letterkenny, Buncrana, Raphoe and Convoy in 1918: 'Their membership tends to increase and their attitude to be more organized and aggressive. There have been strikes, generally rapidly settled by concessions from employers. The demands do not appear really excessive in view of the higher cost of living to non-producers'.[30] The north was distinctive too in that its wages movement matured earlier, and most obviously so in agriculture. Spearheading its drive into Donegal, the NAUL had a branch in Newtowncunningham as early as January 1916, a year before the introduction of compulsory tillage orders and the Agricultural Wages Board tilted the balance of bargaining power in favour of the labourers. The branch, no. 288, catered for farm labourers and flax scutchers. By August 1917, the NAUL was leading strikes around Raphoe, Castlefin, Clady, St Johnston and Ballindrait. As in the south, farm strikes were frequently violent, and touring pickets calling out men still at work were fired on. During another harvest strike in 1918, milk-carts moving into Derry were stopped, prompting farmers to denounce their labourers as 'field Bolsheviks'. In April 1919, the Laggan was convulsed by a strike of over 1,000 farm labourers for higher wages and shorter hours, led by the NAUL. The Workers' Union brought out a similar number in Co. Down. In both areas, farmers confronted pickets with shotguns, and severely checked agricultural trade unionism in Ulster. Many of the strikers did not get their jobs back. The NAUL never attempted another farm strike, preferring to lobby local authorities and the Agricultural Wages Board and bring the law against farmers who paid under the legal minimum rate. By contrast, the ITGWU's presence in southern agriculture was still gaining momentum and would continue until the end of 1923.[31]

Three days after Britain went to war, the NUDL's executive and officials instructed members to give every assistance to the government and observe an industrial truce. The policy was sustained for the duration, and the union collaborated in efforts to raise productivity. James Sexton received a CBE for his contribution to the war effort in 1917. Nonetheless, the union regularly submitted wage claims to keep pace with inflation, rank-and-file hostility to Sexton intensified, unofficial disputes became more common, and there were at least three wage strikes by Derry dockers during the war. To restore the authority of officialdom, the union decided to move towards national pay bargaining, and endorsed the National Transport Workers' Federation's demand for an extra 8*d*. per hour in 1918. One of the four NUDL men on the Federation's negotiation team was Patrick Mallet from Walker's Place.[32]

The other big British-based transport union in Derry, the Amalgamated Society of Railway Servants, had merged with two small societies in 1913 to become the NUR. Irish NUR men played a critical role in challenging wage restraint in 1916, and were the Irish equivalent of Britain's munitions workers in that respect. Most railwaymen earned under 14*s*. per week, and when Ireland's 32 railway companies pleaded inability to increase rates, the threat of a national rail strike compelled the government to bring them under state control and award a 7*s*. per week war bonus. Membership of the NUR in Ireland soared from 4,500 at the end of 1916 to nearly 17,000 by September 1917, including 275 in Derry. With smaller numbers in the Railway Clerks' Association and craft unions, some 80 per cent of railwaymen were now unionized, and the figures suggest the proportion in Derry was higher. Inter-union sectionalism and grade distinctions remained a source of grievance, as the following ditty in the NUR's monthly, the *New Way,* suggests:

> Oh, a Foreman's life in Derry,
> Is more than usually merry,
> With its chances of an extra Special Trip.
> But the prospects of a Fireman,
> Are enough to raise one's ire, man,
> Or, as the vulgar say, give anyone the pip.
> He may sit for his exam,
> But no one gives a damn,
> As to whether for a Driver he is fit
> But if the Firemen got together
> They would quickly find out whether
> The righting of their wrongs passed human wit.[33]

Drivers and firemen had been demanding that the Board of Trade recognize their skill with certificates of competency, which, they felt, would give them a degree of protection in investigation of accidents. For their part, the lower grades looked coldly on the idea of special legislation for the elite footplate men. A motion for certificates was opposed by the NUR and rejected overwhelmingly at the 1919 ITUC.[34]

The growth of trade unionism generally was reflected in the steady advance of Derry trades council. Affiliations rose from 15 in June 1916 to 23 in July 1917 – representing over 2,000 workers – and 28 in September. Delegates in June 1918 included two men from the local branch of the National Association of Discharged Sailors and Soldiers. Formed in 1917, the Association cultivated links with the Labour movement before moving to the right after 1919 and merging into the British Legion.[35] The trades council was also reaching beyond traditional manual sectors to groups like asylum workers, teachers and clerks. Among the wonders of the age was 'the novel spectacle of well-dressed young men and women' distributing leaflets during a shop assistants' strike in 1918. Indeed they went further than the National Union of Shop Assistants, Warehousemen and Clerks could approve in mobbing a manager on his way home.[36] As with the ITUC, the circumstances of war broadened the role of the trades council, leading it to engagement with the establishment of a co-operative society and nominate members to the local Food Control Committee in 1917. Railwaymen were to the fore in promoting co-operatives as a means of combatting profiteering in 1917, and dockers joined the NUDL's embargo on bacon and butter exports in 1920, following the government's promise to decontrol food prices. Even the *Londonderry Sentinel* applauded the dockers. The consolidation of Labour's sense of itself as a social movement is evident in the

Table 1. Wage increases for building workers in Derry city, 1917–20

	Workers affected	*Increase*
1917		
1 May	Carpenters, joiners, bricklayers	8*d.* to 9*d.* per hour
2 July	Painters	½*d.* per hour and a war bonus of 2*s.* per week
17 Aug.	Builders' labourers	22*s.* per week or 24*s.* per week to 5¾*d.* per hour
1918		
1 Jan.	Plumbers	9*d.* to 10*d.* per hour
Sept.	Painters	5*s.* per week in war wages
1919		
1 Apr.	Painters	10*d.* to 1*s.* 3*d.* per hour, merged with a former bonus
9 July	Bricklayers, carpenters, plasterers	1*s.* 6*d.* to 1*s.* 6¾*d.* per hour
28 Sept.	Plumbers	6*s.* 6*d.* per week
	Woodworkers	6*s.* per week
	Sawyers	7*s.* per week
Dec.	Qualified electricians	Uniform rates adopted
1920		
1 Mar.	Painters	1*s.* 3*d.* to 1*s.* 6*d.* per hour, reduction of hours from 50 to 47 per week
1 May	Building labourers	1*s.* to 1*s.* 2*d.* per hour
1 June	Bricklayers	1*s.* 9½*d.* to 2*s.* 0½*d.* per hour
Aug.	Building tradesmen	2*s.* 0½*d.* to 2*s.* 1½*d* per hour

Source: *Labour Gazette*, 1917–21.

trades council's decision to organize a Christmas dance in the Guildhall in 1919 and mark May Day 1920 with a programme of athletics for men and women at the Brandywell on the following Saturday.[37] Reflecting its more regional status, extending to Letterkenny, Strabane and the farms and rural employment in between, the council now styled itself Derry and District Trades and Labour Council; councils in Ulster were less likely that their southern counterparts to discard 'trades and labour' for the common name of 'workers'. Impressive as the expansion was, it is hard to credit the council's affiliation level of 10,000 workers to the ITUC in 1920: the corresponding figures for Belfast and Dublin were 15,000 and 25,000, respectively.[38] It was not unknown for councils to exaggerate membership to Congress for prestige purposes when flush or self-confident, and there was no doubting Labour's swagger in early 1920.

The war years and after were remarkable for the frequency and diversity of wage movements, as demands for changes in rates of pay were called; so much so that by 1919 it was common to refer to 'the wages movement'. An illustration of the wage inflation is found in pay rises gazetted for building workers in Derry (Table 1).

Equally remarkable was the number of strikes (Table 2). The pattern of industrial conflict reflected the evolution of bargaining power. Those of greater relevance to the war economy, notably skilled men in the shipyard, dominated strikes up to 1917. The post-war years saw an extraordinary diffusion of conflict to workers as diverse as mineral water bottlers, printers and biscuit packers. May 1919 saw the greatest number of disputes, with stoppages of building workers, cabinet makers, upholsters, french polishers, caulkers, rivetters, plumbers and railway labourers.

Table 2. Strikes, strikers and strike-days in Derry city, 1914–20

	1914	1915	1916	1917	1918	1919	1920
Strikes	4	6	8	7	16	17	11
Strikers							
Directly involved	989	338	447	633	1,687	969	1,264
Indirectly involved	122			4,998	739	297	17,120
Strike-days	Not available				14,007	28,295	502,038[39]

Source: TNA, Ministry of Labour records, LAB 34/14–20, LAB 34/32–38.

The vast majority of strikes were for wage increases, and the success rate was relatively high, with only 16 of 69 recorded disputes between 1914 and 1920 deemed 'unsuccessful'. Nor do the files record the full extent of conflict. Officials missed the smaller Irish strikes on occasion, and took no account of alternative methods of industrial struggle. Ca'canny, a Scottish form of sabotage, best described as 'bad work for bad pay', was rumoured to be rife in the shipyard in 1919. One yardman, a 19-year-old with three years' service in the army, appeared in court for assaulting an apprentice caulker for 'working too hard'.[40]

The social consequences of disputes could be pitiful where essentials like bread and coal were affected. During a stoppage of dockers and carters in the 'arctic' spring of 1919, crowds gathered on the quay, expecting emergency rations of fuel from the Coal Controller. But when bellmen refused to do the work of carters, the merchants refused to release the coal. After eyeing the black diamonds from a distance:

some of the more venturesome produced bags and began to fill them. In less than half an hour there was a regular scramble, men, women, and children swarming unto the piles of coal like ants. Those returning with well-filled bags to their homes spread like wildfire the news of the raid, and gradually the crowd of raiders swelled, coming from the poorer quarters of the city. Bags, baskets, buckets, and haversacks were requisitioned to hold the coal. During a heavy hailstorm these were quickly filled, and in an incredibly short space of time there appeared on the scene trucks, donkey carts, barrows, a lorry, and even a hackney car, all of which were sent away well laden. For several hours this extraordinary operation continued with the Harbour constables and a number of the Royal Irish Constabulary looking on. Soldiers in uniform and silver badge men [discharged, wounded veterans] were among those who filled and carried way bags.[41]

Seventy-five summonses for larceny were issued.[42]

Could the strike wave have transformed northern Labour ideologically, as it did in the south? As diplomats gathered in Paris for the peace talks that were supposed to create a new, democratic world, it seemed a possibility. On 25 January 1919, 30,000 engineering and shipbuilding workers in Belfast struck unofficially for a 44-hour week. The unrest spread to municipal employees, and command of power supplies gave the strike committee some administrative authority, prompting journalists to write of 'the Belfast soviet'. Derry officials of the Federation of Engineering and Shipbuilding Trades invited all workers to the Guildhall on 3 February to discuss their response. Shy of asking bluntly for a sympathetic strike, they proposed that Derry unions levy members to help Belfast and notice all local employers for a 44-hour week by 1 May. When Thomas Cassidy rose to speak, his presence was challenged, and he said he was there as 'a worker in Derry'. In fact, Cassidy was chairman of the ITUC executive, and argued that action had to be national, and that an ITUC conference was due to meet on 8 February to discuss the formation of a national movement for a 44-hour week and a 50s. per week minimum wage. But what was 'national'? The metal trades in Belfast, and many in Derry too, wanted little to do with Dublin. The hours movement had developed in British shipbuilding. Belfast had already rejected offers of help from the ITUC and ITGWU, both of which were now openly identifying with Sinn Féin. After lively exchanges, the meeting adopted an amendment that Derry workers be balloted on a 44-hours movement. Despite the best efforts of the 'Belfast soviet' to keep the dispute moderate, a-political, and parochial, Dublin Castle was becoming alarmed at the contagion of 'Bolshevism' and the prospect of Sinn Féin winning Protestant support through it. Soldiers took over the gasworks and electricity station on 14 February, and the strike collapsed before Derry could take action.[43] Herein lay the dilemma for northern Labour. Any form of radicalism left it open to being bracketed with revolution and nationalism.

POLITICS

Politically, Derry straddled the divide between British and Irish Labour. New unionism had brought it into the orbit of the amalgamateds. When Larkin founded an Irish union, the NUDL branch and leading officials on the trades council denounced him. As the challenge from the ITUC and the ITGWU grew ever more vigorous after 1917, the city's response to the rise of Irish Labour became more ambivalent. The ITUC was being drawn deeper into politics since the third Home Rule crisis. It chose not to meet in 1915 because of the war, and its first wartime Congress, in Sligo in August 1916, was also its first after the Easter Rising. Both Cassidy and James McCarron spoke in favour of a motion opposing partition, a possibility denounced overwhelmingly by Congress in 1914. 'The Home Rule Act must be passed', added Cassidy, 'and whoever was against it must face the consequences'. The Congress confirmed his standing as the leading Derry Labourite. He was now 43 years old, married with five daughters and one son, and living at 41 Chapel Road on the Waterside. His return to the 1911 census said he could speak Irish. The census was the first in which significant numbers made the claim as a gesture of support for Irish-Ireland. Cassidy topped the poll in the elections to the executive, and the delegates agreed that the 1917 Congress should be in Derry.[44]

The Sligo Congress is remembered for the way it trod gingerly around the contentions of the day. The Derry Congress would not be so inhibited. In May the trades council hosted a 'fairly large' preparatory meeting in the Guildhall. Revd Bruce Wallace cabled a message of solidarity from Limavady.[45] The Congress opened in the Guildhall at 11a.m. on Monday, 6 August. One-hundred-and-twenty attended, 18 of them from Derry: four from the trades council, three from the ASTT, two each from the NUDL, the NAUL and the Typographical Association, and one each from the Amalgamated Society of Engineers, the National Sailors' and Firemen's Union, the Railway Clerks' Association, the Shirt and Collar Cutters' Union, and the Ancient Guild of Incorporated Brick and Stone Layers. Despite the widening rift between Labour and Unionism nationally, Mayor Anderson was present in his regalia to welcome the gathering. That afternoon the delegates enjoyed a brake drive to Buncrana, where the mayor provided refreshments in Saint Mary's Hall. On Tuesday night they were treated to a trades council banquet in the Guildhall and were guests of Barney Armstrong at his opera house. The programme featured a scene from the delightful 'Maritana', a comedian, a 'surprise', a banjo player, 'two blind girls in musical artistry' and a singer in 'a picturesque Irish scena'. A number of the visitors stayed over on the Wednesday night to attend a meeting of the P.H. Pearse Sinn Féin cumann in the Gaelic League Hall in Richmond Street, and call for national unity and independence. The Congress debates revealed the emerging divide on the war and the constitutional question. The most heated discussion arose over the ITUC executive's decision to send two representatives to the proposed socialist peace conference at Stockholm. Moreover, the Irish duo at Stockholm would be mandated 'to seek to establish the Irish labour party as a distinct unit in the International Labour Movement', and endorse the recent All-Russian Congress of Soviets of Workers' and Soldiers' Deputies in its call for peace without annexations or indemnities. To 'loud and prolonged' applause, the trip to Stockholm was approved of by 68–24 votes. McCarron and Councillor William Logue, president of the trades council, a typographer with the *Derry Journal*, and later a NAUL organizer, spoke against it. Both McCarron and Logue were pro-war. Cassidy spoke in favour. A further controversy arose over Tom McPartlin's presidential address, which Unionist newspapers condemned for advocating class war.[46]

It was 1918 before Derry trades council fell in step with southern Labour in embracing socialism and a stance on the war that varied from critical to hostile. Conscription could be seen as a Labour issue, having been opposed by Labour in Britain and Australia. It would meet determined resistance in Canada too. In Ireland, the ITUC issued a manifesto in November 1916 with two negative demands, no partition and no conscription, and staged its first general strike, against the Military Service Act, on 23 April.[47] Despite its Labour credentials, and some Unionist support, opposition to conscription was identified with nationalism. After the Derry NUR passed a resolution against the Military Service Act, in line with union policy in Britain, Unionist railwaymen published a protest in the *Londonderry Sentinel*. The general strike itself was not widespread in Ulster. In Derry, the dockers, carters, and some shipyard and engineering workers came out. In Belfast, only the Catholic schools closed.[48] Derry trades council did not broach the subject until June. Logue persuaded the pro-Union elements that it was purely a Labour question, and for the sake of unity it suited them to agree. On a vote of 33–1, with two men present from the National Association of Discharged Sailors and Soldiers, the council deplored the Military Service Act.[49]

Cassidy was at one with the Dublin leadership throughout these years. Vice-chairman of the ITUC in 1917 and chairman in 1918, he presided over historic decisions, such as the famous special conference on 1 November 1918 at which Labour decided to withdraw from the forthcoming general election, and his nondescript role has gone unnoticed. The neglect is not unfair. Even in Derry, Logue was the more influential. Logue was gradually shifting his position. At the special conference he welcomed the executive's recommendation to stand down from the election, a move seen to benefit Sinn Féin, arguing that Labour candidates would divide the nationalist vote.[50] McCarron, on the other hand, grew increasingly estranged from the trajectory of Labour. At the 1917 Congress he had opposed a motion for a Federation of Labour, saying it 'would mean the wiping out of amalgamated societies in this country'. The resolution was referred to the executive. He then defied Congress in taking a seat in the Irish Convention. Seven of the 95 seats were reserved for Labour, but the ITUC

4. James McCarron's
memorial headstone
in the City Cemetery,
Derry.

and southern trades councils boycotted what was perceived as a government manoeuvre to impose devolution rather than grant self-determination. McCarron was joined by a Dublin NUR man and three from Belfast trades council. All five Labour men signed the Convention's majority report, favouring dominion Home Rule.[51] At the 1918 Congress he challenged the credentials of William O'Brien, de facto chief of the ITGWU and the most powerful man in the Labour movement, claiming that O'Brien had been expelled from the ASTT. The challenge was dismissed by 159 to 38 votes.[52] McCarron would soon be Derry trades council's most notable casualty of the war, lost with the mailboat *Leinster* on 10 October en route to a union meeting in London. In death he united socialists and policemen, republicans and Unionists. The lord mayor of Dublin intervened to secure a coffin – the city's undertakers being struck – and ITUC leaders and a large contingent of ITGWU men escorted the remains to the Great Northern terminus at Amiens Street. P.T. Daly, McCarron's old sparring partner in Congress, rode with him to Foyle Road, where hundreds waited with Mayor Anderson. McCarron's son, Joseph, was a private in the Royal Irish Fusiliers and RIC men took a lift of the coffin. A film of the vast funeral cortège was shown in Saint Columb's Hall, and in March 1920 a 12-foot high limestone Celtic cross was erected in McCarron's memory in the City

Cemetery by 'leading citizens and trade union organizations as an appreciation of his life-work' (fig. 4).[53]

The Sinn Féin landslide in the 1918 general election displaced ambiguity with open association between Labour and republicans. In compliance with a recommendation of the international socialist conference at Berne, Switzerland, in February 1919, the ITUC called a 'general holiday' for international proletarian solidarity and national self-determination on 1 May. Derry trades council planned a march from the Mall Wall to the Waterside and back to a rally at Tinney's field on the Strand Road. Three bands were engaged. The 'No Surrender' band – loyalist, we presume – declined an invitation. Unionists had meanwhile created an alternative to official Labour in the Ulster Unionist Labour Association (UULA). Aside from the nagging fear of Labour enticing Protestant workers to republicanism, Carson especially was nervous of the social ramifications of Labour power in the post-war world. Three UULA MPs were elected, in Belfast, in the 1918 election. The Londonderry UULA was formed, comparatively late, in February 1919. Led by Mayor Anderson, who owned hosiery and knitting factories in Derry and Gweedore, it aimed to advance Unionism, maintain the Unionist majority on the Corporation, form a Unionist employment bureau, and foster harmony between Unionist employers and employees. One of its first initiatives was to meet local Unionist employers, and it acquired a notoriety for being more jealously Protestant than the Unionist Party where jobs were at stake. A future chairman, Alderman John Mark, assured electors that his brother, a bacon-curer in Foyle Street, employed no nationalists.[54] In February it undertook a canvass in 'several' factories, and in April it appealed to Protestants not to join the May Day parade as it was 'of a revolutionary and Bolshevik nature and supported by Sinn Féin'. On the day, the walls were occupied by troops and the parade was proclaimed. Hundreds milled about the streets until driven indoors by showers. Catholic schools had closed, Protestant schools stayed open.[55] There had been resignations from the Irish National Teachers' Organization executive in protest at its support for the anti-conscription strike and affiliation to the ITUC. A self-styled Londonderry Teachers' Association disaffiliated in December 1918. In 1919, the Irish National Teachers' Organization noted the loss of four branches, in Derry, Coleraine, Lisburn and Newtownards, and the subsequent formation of the Ulster Teachers' Union. The Association of Secondary Teachers, Ireland also lost Protestant members on its affiliation to Congress in 1920. In both cases, substantial numbers of Protestant teachers stayed with the unions concerned.[56] An Ulster Workers' Trade Union was founded also, for general workers, but met firm opposition from other unions and made no impact in Derry.[57] The mutual alienation of Labour and Unionism intensified over the following year. In November 1919, the trades council was outraged to discover that the Corporation had allocated three of the five 'labour' seats on the local War Pensions Committee to the UULA.[58]

The municipal elections in January 1920 saw the city starkly divided. Held under proportional representation, the hustings were fiercely contested as nationalists hoped for a majority. Nineteen Unionists, 11 Nationalists, and 10 Sinn Féiners were returned, and the election of the first Catholic mayor since 1688 produced outbursts of 'God save Ireland' and 'Amhrán na bhFiann' in the Guildhall. The trades council had resolved to run candidates, only for 'difficulties' to ensure that trades council activists stood as Nationalists or Sinn Féiners, while the Unionists fielded UULA men, led by Henry Greenway, soon to be chairman of the local branch of the Union of Postal Workers (Table 3).[59]

Table 3. Candidates with working class occupations in the municipal elections, 1920

Ward	seats	Unionists (working class)	Nationalists (working class)	Sinn Féin (working class)
North	11	8 (Henry Greenway, postman)	3 (-)	2 (Edward McCafferty, engineer)
South and east	12	8 (David Mitchell, tailor)	3 (W.J. Bradley, postman, Con Doherty, tailor)	3 (Robert McAnaney, tailor, James Gallagher, plater's helper)
Waterside	9	7 (James Blair, plumber, D.P. Thompson, compositor)	2 (-)	2 (-)
West	8	-	4 (William Logue, labour organizer [NAUL], Joseph McKernan, merchant seaman, Patrick Meenan, labour delegate [NUDL])	4 (Anthony Carlin, house painter)

Source: *Derry Journal*, 7 Jan. 1920.

Other than Mitchell, all of the working-class candidates were elected. But the muddy status of 'Labour' continued. Once again, Derry was the only city in Ireland without designated Labour councillors, and no love was lost between Greenway, Blair and Thompson, and their 'so-called Labour Association' and the Labour nationalist councillors.[60]

Labour support for the independence campaign reached its apogee in two further actions, the political prisoners' strike and the railway munitions strike. On Monday, 12 April, the Congress executive called an immediate, indefinite general strike for the release of 100 republicans on hunger strike in Mountjoy. As yet, few understood how long a total fast could last. The daily expectation of death wound up an unbearable tension. Derry trades council met on Tuesday night and called for industrial action in non-essential services from Wednesday. Dockers, most carters, Corporation bus crews, some shipyardmen, and teachers in Catholic schools responded.[61] Nationally, the stoppage climaxed in spectacular success when Dublin Castle took fright at what it saw as the 'Bolshevist' turn of the revolution and freed the hunger strikers at 4p.m. on Wednesday. The other significant Labour contribution originated in May 1920 with railway dockers at Dublin's North Wall refusing to handle British army munitions.[62] The boycott gradually spread to dockers and railwaymen throughout nationalist areas. As the NUR's British leadership tried to moderate the protest, the ITUC stepped in with financial assistance. Congress avoided strike action as such, leaving it up to the British military to force the issue. And force it they did. Derry dockers were quick to respond. On 14 July, the *Derry Standard* noted that the refusal of a driver on the Londonderry and Lough Swilly Railway to move a train carrying troops was the first such incident in the north. By the end of the month 30 railwaymen on the Lough Swilly had been suspended for similar action. The Derry NUR branch resolved:

> That we, the representatives of the majority of the employees of the Lough Swilly Railway ... wish it to be clearly understood that under no circumstances will we convey or assist in the conveyance of armed military or police to be utilized for the destruction of our fellow-countrymen. We absolutely refuse to be party to the creation of a second Amritzar.[63]

The massacre of Punjabis at Amritsar carried a particular meaning in Ulster. Carson was a well-known apologist for General Reginald Dyer, who directed the slaughter. Days earlier, a 'well-attended meeting' of all grades at the Waterside Station had pledged support to the government and the railway companies in transporting munitions and troops.[64] In September the disruption extended to the Donegal Railway. On 14 December, with over 500 men dismissed, and the economy severely affected, Congress recommended an end to the protest. Aside from being 'a serious set-back to military actions', in the words of the British commander-in-chief in Ireland, General Neville Macready, it had compelled the NUR to summon a meeting of the British Trades Union Congress that condemned the military occupation. The NUR had issued strike pay to unemployed members who had not contravened management orders, and was largely successful in getting the men their jobs back. The railway companies quietly accepted the return to work with little victimization.[65] Their agonies, west of the Foyle at any rate, were far from over as republican sabotage of track, locomotives, points and signals intensified up to the height of the Civil War.

As it puzzled over its sluggish advance across the Boyne, the ITGWU's *Voice of Labour* started a debate, exceptional in the annals of contemporary Labour, on the mentality of Ulster workers and their differences with the south. The *Voice*'s editor, Cathal O'Shannon, had been raised in Draperstown and a scholarship boy at Saint Columb's, Derry. 'Workers in the "south and west"', wrote O'Shannon, trailing his coat across the front page,

> have long been accustomed to think of Belfast as an industrial Oxford – the home of lost causes, unreasoning conservatism, political and social, with a hopelessly parochial outlook. Their loyalty to trade unionism has been unquestioned, but they have entertained, long after the British worker had abandoned it, the view of trade unionism as a merely protective instrument.

Logue responded, saying that trade unionism in Ulster had 'in large measure succeeded', and could compare favourably with any part of the United Kingdom. He conceded that in politics the picture was not so bright due to northern 'suspicions', but was optimistic that 'we are gradually emerging into that position when we fully realise our strength'.[66] The early 1920s would show his optimism to be cruelly misplaced. Wage militancy did not translate easily into class politics in divided Ulster. But it could have some impact. With no alternative other than 'yellow' unions like the Ulster Workers' Trade Union or lapdogs like the UULA, Unionist workers tholed Labour nationalism where they had to. British unions like the NUDL and NUR accommodated republicanism, however grudgingly, to retain their Irish members, who in turn were prepared to accept British unions as long as they delivered on wages. It was when the British failed to deliver that the ITGWU, and one Peadar O'Donnell, would get its chance.

3. Slump, 1920–3

Massive expansion of the world's productive capacity led to a crisis of overproduction in the summer of 1920. The North's traditional industries were badly hit. In June 1921, out of 260,000 insured workers in Northern Ireland, 65,507 were idle and 43,575 were on short-time. The insurance acts excluded farm labourers and domestic servants, who were experiencing unemployment rates at least as high. Derry city had 3,884 people idle in late 1921, including 2,336 men, 1,335 women, 45 boys and 128 girls. By 1923, female unemployment had halved, but the figure for men had hardly changed. Male employment prospects would suffer long-term blows from the closure of Watt's distilleries and the North of Ireland Shipbuilding Company. Cheaper consumer prices partly compensated for falling wages. The cost of living index, weighted at 100 in July 1914, peaked at 276 in November 1920, and dropped to a low of 169 in March 1923.[1] Employers pushed for a return to pre-1914 wage levels. Paralleling the economic crisis, a related political nightmare unfolded, though the nature of the relationship is questioned. Within days of the election of a Nationalist mayor, the Dorsetshire regiment and the RIC raided homes in Derry, seizing munitions and 'seditious' literature. Clashes with the Dorsets and inter-communal violence erupted during the political prisoners strike in April 1920, and the Irish Republican Army (IRA) launched its first attack on the RIC in Derry, at Lecky Road barracks, on 16 April. The tensions exploded lethally in June. Forty people died in the disturbances, 19 of them in what the *Londonderry Sentinel* called 'civil war week' in June. A heavy military intervention on 23 June curbed the shooting, but not the inter-communal strife. The Dorsets' behaviour became blatantly partisan, to the point where RIC men resigned in protest at the regiment's collaboration with the Ulster Volunteer Force. Their dissent was trumped by the creation of the Special Constabulary in October 1920.[2] Sources suggest that there were elements in the paramilitaries on both sides who tried to contain the violence, and ultimately the nationalists' reluctance to confront the superior firepower and military cohesion of the Unionists and the British army settled the issue.

Events intensified the nexus of Labour and the national question. In July 1920, Belfast loyalists drove over 8,000 workers from their jobs, almost a quarter of them Protestants targeted for their Labour politics. Nationalist Ireland retaliated with a boycott of Belfast goods, co-ordinated by Dáil Éireann's Department of Labour and backed by the ITUC.[3] Week after week the *Derry Journal* published lists of subscriptions to the expellees' distress fund, while the

Londonderry Sentinel took to citing Congress as 'Sinn Féin Labour'. In Derry, the intersection of Labour and nationalism is encapsulated in the story of Peadar O'Donnell and the ITGWU. From August 1920, O'Donnell launched an offensive against the amalgamateds. By 1921, the ITGWU in the rest of Ireland was following suit, projecting itself as the OBU and the steadfast alternative to the crumbling British unions. There was a foundation to the propaganda. Initially, unions had pledged to 'hold the harvest' of wage gains and tolerate no going back to pre-1914 conditions. Britain's 'Black Friday', 15 April 1921, when the 'triple alliance' of miners, the NUR and the National Transport Workers' Federation, collapsed and left the miners to their fate, was the signal for a general assault on wages. The year 1920 'was remarkable for the unprecedented depression in trade and commerce which set in with great suddenness which set in during the autumn', the president of Derry Chamber of Commerce told colleagues.

> It was not too much to say that on the outcome of the present miners' dispute hung the prosperity of all classes for the future … unless cheaper labour could be obtained the outlook was black … it was to be hoped that Labour would realise the impossibility of maintaining the high wages brought about by war conditions, and the refusal of the Triple Alliance to support the miners was a favourable sign.[4]

Of 27 wage strikes in Northern Ireland in 1921, 23 were directed against reductions. Taking advantage of the unsettled conditions in the south, where effective policing was not introduced until after the Civil War, Irish unions fared better for longer. About half of ITGWU members still retained peak rates at the end of 1922.[5] In these circumstances, the Derry ITGWU could make grinding progress.

PARTITION

The Government of Ireland Act became law in December 1920, and the process of separating the six and 26 counties was first brought home to people with the realignment of poor law unions straddling county boundaries that were destined to become international frontiers. Partition infused events with a lethal importance. Holding the balance of power on the Corporation, the Nationalists moderated Sinn Féin policy, declining to pledge allegiance to Dáil Éireann, and trusting the 'Lilliput state' would prove unworkable or that the Saorstát government would get the Boundary Commission to push the border east. Unionists counter-mobilized. The 'Labour' councillors were prominent on all sides of the debate, and trade unions were caught in the crossfire, sometimes literally. Twenty bullets perforated a window in the NUDL office in Butcher

Street in October 1920, and the military raided the ITGWU office in William Street in January 1921.[6]

The new political geography saw the city lose twice over. The perception of Northern Ireland as a Belfast-anchored city-state made Derry more peripheral within the six counties, while customs, tariffs, paperwork and delays eroded its utility as a distribution centre for Donegal. Partition entailed a reconfiguration, too, of industrial relations. As the Corporation had never recognized the Republic, Dáil Éireann's Department of Labour arbitration courts never functioned in Derry, as they did in Donegal. But there was plenty of other business to be dealt with in determining the future of the extraordinary structures generated by the First World War, notably state control of the railways, the Agricultural Wages Board, and trade boards. Northern Ireland's Ministry of Labour began to take over the functions of Britain's Department of Labour in Dublin and establish its own conciliation services from May 1921. Trade unionists were apprehensive. Aside from the Unionist suspicion that all shades of the Labour movement were anti-partitionist, 20 of the 40 Unionist MPs were company directors or merchants, three were landowners, 10 were professionals, and the four working-class MPs thought their only reliable colleagues were in the UULA or 'Ulster' trade unions. Westminster transferred trade boards to the remit of the Ministry of Labour in late 1921/early 1922 and employers lobbied the minister, J.M. Andrews, chairman of the UULA and a linen manufacturer, to dispense with them. Fortunately for Northern Ireland, Andrews and the cabinet believed in 'step by step', i.e. tracking Westminster legislation to maintain parity of treatment with Britain. Pennies were pinched where possible. Andrews' Trade Boards Act (1923) discontinued the flax and hemp board, slashing the numbers covered by boards from 115,000 to 51,000, minimized the role of the state in wage negotiation, and had more in common with the 1909 Trade Boards Act than the 1918 Act. Rates set by the boards provided for a subsistence living and declined steadily from 1924 to 1935. The key board for Derry, shirtmaking, covered 6,000 workers.[7] The government also decontrolled the railways and scrapped the Agricultural Wages Board.

There were a few cases of resistance to the Northern regime until economic pressures prevailed. The ITGWU urged workers to maintain all-Ireland wage bargaining, and dockers and railwaymen remained within all-Ireland agreements up to 1922–3. In December 1922, Belfast loco men demanded that wage proposals apply to all NUR men in Ireland.[8] In education, highly sensitive because of the Catholic Church's antagonism to the 'Belfast junta', about one-third of Catholic schools refused to recognize Northern Ireland and had their teachers paid by the Provisional government in Dublin until October 1922. Derry Corporation's non-recognition of the Belfast government meant it ran out of funds for unemployment relief in 1922.[9] The abolition of proportional representation and revision of wards was expected to restore a Unionist majority on the Corporation in January 1923. Nationalists boycotted the elections.

'THE REVOLUTION IS COMING': THE RISE OF THE OBU

After its battering in the 1913 lockout and the dislocation of Easter Week, the ITGWU recovered rapidly in the south in 1917. In Ulster, where the amalgamateds were entrenched, the NAUL and Workers' Union had stolen a march on Liberty Hall and the union's socialist republicanism was not so popular. Not until January 1919 did Peadar O'Donnell arrive in the city, lodging with a Gweedore man in Waterloo Street. The ITGWU branch he founded (no. 179) was based on employees in the city's four cinemas, and James Houston, Bishop Street, became secretary. Another branch in Clady Urney (no. 420) was launched in December 1919.[10] Born in the Rosses in 1893, O'Donnell qualified as a primary teacher in 1913, and got active in union work in 1918, affiliating the Gweedore and Rosses Irish National Teachers' Organization to the Derry trades council and going to Scotland on behalf of the tattie hookers. After joining the ITGWU's staff in 1918 and reading himself into 'a very convinced Marxist', he acquired a reputation as one of the union's most enterprising agitators. Famously, he won a strike in Monaghan Lunatic Asylum by hoisting a red flag over the hospital and declaring a 'soviet'. Within weeks of the ITGWU's establishment in Derry, the *Derry Journal*, with its usual mix of sympathy for mainstream Labour and untiring animosity to socialism as irreligious, editorialized on the presence of 'avowedly revolutionary' elements 'discarding the application of Christian principles'. In the first of a series of letters to the press, O'Donnell assured the *Journal*: 'The revolution is coming'.[11] The exchange would be characteristic of the spats that dogged his career in the city. While he sometimes lodged with Edward McCafferty, Amalgamated Society of Engineers, secretary of the trades council, and a Sinn Féin councillor in 1920, at 11 Northland Avenue, his relations with the trades council and the British unions were not so cordial. O'Donnell made no secret of his Connollyite politics and strained to link the ITGWU with the independence struggle. In February 1920, he and McCafferty formed a Workers' Education Committee, intended as the nucleus of a branch of the James Connolly College in Dublin, to offer courses in economics and industrial history. The Committee's first public lecturer was the city's Sinn Féin MP, Eoin MacNeill, who spoke to a sizable attendance in the Guildhall on the co-operative commonwealth.[12] Nominated for the Poor Law Guardians in April, O'Donnell listed his occupation as 'Workers' Republican Organizer'. He also urged the continuation of the railway munitions strike and solidarity with Terence MacSwiney's hunger strike, which held the world's attention in late 1920.[13] The amalgamated dominated trades council decided that there was no need for the ITGWU in Derry and denied it affiliation.[14]

The historians' verdict on O'Donnell and the ITGWU is negative. He has been accused of recruiting no more than a handful of workers, and these on the basis of an appeal to 'Catholic nationalism', faulted for descending to Anglophobic attacks on the amalgamateds, and blamed for the demise of Watt's distilleries in Derry. 'He left a trail of broken unions and industrial closure behind him', according to the pro-establishment *Atlantic gateway*. Radical historians have been none too complimentary either. Even O'Donnell himself was rueful, telling interviewers in the 1980s that he regarded his intervention in the city as unnecessary and divisive. His problems of man-management as commandant of the local IRA may also have soured his memory, and he does seem to have had a talent for making enemies, with easygoing Derrymen at any rate. The IRA resented his efforts to recruit for the Citizen Army and determination to bundle them into a more active role, while the ITGWU was apprehensive about IRA meetings on its premises. Derry is treated *en passant* in O'Donnell's recollections.[15] Yet the arraignments are not well founded, and are skewed by O'Donnell's proclivity in old age to deprecate his early activism, a common enough characteristic of veterans reminiscing on a lifetime of swimming vainly against the current for values near incomprehensible to younger generations. It is hard to reconcile O'Donnell's regret about confronting the amalgamateds with his observation in 1985 that their officials were infected by the 'vapid socialism characteristic of the British Labour movement'.[16]

O'Donnell's work was not confined to Derry and in 1920 alone he led strikes in Donegal Town and Cootehill, and reformed the Armagh city branch of the ITGWU, again.[17] According to the RIC, the Derry branch had a trifling 25 members up to August 1920, when it 'made an individual canvas throughout all centres of industry' and membership rose incrementally, to 315 by September 1921. Undoubtedly, membership was well below that in southern cities – the union had 45 branches and 7,738 members in Limerick city and county – but the figures may not have been so derisory or progress so incremental.[18] The employers' counter-attack came early to Derry. On 12 June 1920 the UGW, with 286 cutters and apprentices in Derry, struck for a leapfrogging rise of 15s. per week for cutters and 7s. 6d. per week for apprentices after the failure of employers to pass on a wage increase granted to colleagues in Britain. The timing of the strike was unfortunate in that it spanned the economic downturn. The cutters expected the profits boom to deliver a quick result. The Shirt Manufacturers' Federation realized they would soon have a surfeit of stock and took advantage with a general lockout on 16 July, throwing about 7,000 Derry girls out of work. Most were in the ASTT, and in an industry where strikes or lockouts rarely lasted longer than a few days, T.A. Flynn, general secretary of the ASTT, concluded that his union could not afford strike pay. Instead it granted £1,250 to the distress fund, and raised a further £1,800 or so from an appeal to branches in Britain. It was regarded as a modest gesture, given that the UGW donated £2,000 and the girls were losing at least £10,000 per week in wages. Reporting from Derry, Flynn was scathing about the UGW, saying its cutters in cross-channel branches of Derry firms were working overtime and endorsing claims, made both by the trades council and the *Londonderry Sentinel*, that it was trying to destroy Irish industry.[19] Meanwhile Derry dockers and carters blacked exports from companies in dispute and 'backed us [the cutters] till their nose bled'. The mainly Protestant cutters were impressed.[20]

From new offices in William Street, O'Donnell recruited both factory girls and cutters. Liberty Hall sent £73 10s. to 'Derry Tailoresses' on 27 July.[21] On 4 August, hundreds of women protested about the lack of strike pay outside the ASTT's office at 20 Shipquay Street and marched along the Strand to the shipyard singing snatches of songs and shouting 'up Dublin', 'up the rebels'. Either the protest or rumours that the girls were joining the UGW prompted O'Donnell to intervene publicly. That the UGW was currently in merger talks with the Scottish Operative Tailors' and Tailoresses' Association to found the Tailors' and Garment Workers' Union, brought wider questions to the agenda. The Tailors' and Garment Workers' was to be an industrial union, ready to recruit everyone in the trade, and, *parri passu*, was seen as a threat by the ASTT. James Connolly's dismissal of this non-revolutionary industrial unionism as 'old wine in new bottles' and a device to kill the real, revolutionary industrial unionism of the OBU was a pillar of ITGWU propaganda.[22] O'Donnell insisted that he admired the strike. At the same time, he deplored the UGW for its miscalculation, and accused it of selecting Derry for a cheap fight, as a strike in British branches would have meant strike pay for more than the cutters. Only following criticism from O'Donnell that it was 'doing nothing' did the trades council set up a distress fund. O'Donnell also represented cutters in negotiations with the Shirt Manufacturers' Federation. Once the dispute had ended, with the concession of 2s. per week to the cutters, he convened a big ITGWU rally in the Guildhall. 'His position was easy to understand', he said. 'He was in Derry, not to smash the cross-Channel unions catering for the girls, but to smash every cross Channel union in Derry'. Several hundred were reported to have enrolled in the OBU. Cathal O'Shannon applauded in the ITGWU's *Watchword of Labour*, with jibes at 'the harmless Trades Council' and 'the mercenary cross-channel Unions'. The UULA took out large advertisements in the *Sentinel* and the *Derry Standard* urging 'all Protestant workers' to have nothing to do with the ITGWU and to 'get into and remain in their respective Amalgamated Trade Unions'. The UULA also announced that it would be making collections for distressed Protestant strikers, alleging that the trades council was discriminating against Protestants in the disbursal of relief.[23]

O'Donnell had joined the IRA in 1919 and began 'doing odd jobs for one IRA officer or another, picking up revolvers here and there, ferrying arms'. In mid-1920 he assumed command of the 2nd Battalion, Donegal Brigade, whose operational area included Derry city. Warned of an impending arrest by an RIC sergeant in Derry, 'a fervent Unionist' whom he had helped in the setting up of the Police and Prison Officers' Union, he went on the run as a full-time IRA man in November 1920.[24] His short trade union career was over, apart from occasional work for tattie hookers and the Scottish Farm Servants' Union. Like many a revolutionary, he was an agitator rather than an organizer, and found trade unionism 'slow and plodding work'. Charlie Ridgway replaced him.[25] The growth of the ITGWU continued apace, and extended beyond the shirt factories. By April 1921 the branch had sections for engineering and shipbuilding, municipal employees, bottlers, builders' labourers, distillery workers and girls. O'Donnell claimed the dockers had been willing to defect from the NUDL on condition they could bring their secretary, Bill McNulty, with them. O'Donnell had no issue with the terms, and the Belfast branch of the National Sailors' and Firemen's Union would be absorbed in similar style, but head office baulked at McNulty. The girls' section celebrated May Day with a successful concert in the Guildhall. Of the 34 labour bodies asked to contribute to the concert, none replied. Featuring 'the cream of Derry and Dublin talent', the programme opened with uileann pipes and 'the Internationale' – so popular it was given an encore – and closed with 'the Red Flag'. The guest of honour was James Baird, spokesman for the Belfast Expelled Workers' Committee, and himself a former boilermaker in Harland and Wolff. Baird and the Revd Bruce Wallace were among the four 'socialists' who contested the Northern Ireland parliament elections in May. Both finished at the bottom of the poll, Baird winning 875 votes in Belfast East, and Wallace gleaning 926 votes in Belfast North. Ridgway claimed that the ITGWU was now the biggest union catering for Derry's factory girls, and the girls' section was certainly vibrant. In June it organized a picnic in Buncrana and in September it hosted a three-day social and sports carnival in the Brandywell.[26]

The ITGWU was regularly vilified in the Derry press as anti-Catholic (for its socialism), anti-Protestant (for its republicanism), anti-British (for its militant drive against the amalgamateds), and even anti-Derry (on the ground that Ridgway was from Belfast, and a Protestant to boot). It was not alone in being abused. In the febrile atmosphere of the time, there were accusations too of trade union collusion in discrimination against Catholics on the Lough Swilly Railway and speculation about sectarian division in the NUR, charges refuted by the secretaries of the NUR and the Railway Clerks' Association, and, arguably, by their dogged resistance to the cuts that followed decontrol of the railways.[27] But no union suffered as much abuse or encountered as much reaction as the ITGWU. The amalgamateds accused it of exploiting the sectarian and political tensions in the city, and the fact that its membership growth coincided with their failure to defend wages and conditions merely strengthened the determination to isolate it. Not surprisingly, employers too were hostile. The Amalgamated Society of Painters circulated a blacklist of ITGWU men to employers after the Painters lost members in the shipyard. Both the North of Ireland Shipbuilding Company and Watt's victimized ITGWU men.[28]

The most serious charge against O'Donnell, and one he remembered sadly in old age, was that he closed Watt's distilleries.[29] The NAUL had struck Watt's in September 1920 for a wage increase. O'Donnell kept his men at work, citing the ITUC's policy of suspending sectional action to prioritize the railway munitions strike. For O'Donnell the railway protest involved a supreme moral principle, a critical battle in the war against imperialism, and a way of turning the national struggle into a class struggle. If it brought transport to a standstill and 'humping the food on our backs through the fields' so much the better as it would put the revolution in the hands of the people. Organized Labour should prepare for a fight *à l'outrance* by creating a food distribution network, as it planned to do during the political prisoners' strike.[30] Watt's saved the ITGWU's face with a general lockout, but the NAUL accused it of scabbing in any case. In reply, O'Donnell asked which of the unions had the trust of the workforce? The NAUL had 40 men in Watt's while the ITGWU had 130. In June 1921 the ITGWU struck for recognition and against a pay cut. The NAUL accepted Watt's demands, pleading that the alternative was closure.[31] As an observer, ever anxious to fuse the national and social revolutions, O'Donnell interpreted Watt's threat of closure as part of foreign capital's economic war on the nation. His answer was near Maoist. 'No industry', he wrote, 'has a right to exist if it can't pay a living wage'.

> Let the threat of a close down once intimidate the workers to withdraw a demand intelligently decided on and working class organizations shall cease to serve any good purpose … The Irish nation is up against the necessity to scrap old standards and a get sense of real values … Ireland may be blockaded. What are we to do? Beat the blockade. It's easy. Machinery to control the food produced in the country must be summoned into being at once. Money, and money standards, must end for a big section, perhaps ultimately for all.[32]

O'Donnell was given 'a great reception' on Sunday, 17 July, when the Watt's strike committee brought close to 1,000 friends on a walk to An Grianan Aileach for a day of 'health, pleasure, and education', with games, reels and lectures, topped and tailed by 'the Internationale' and 'the Red Flag'. The strike ended in a technical victory for the ITGWU on 27 July.[33] Production stopped in October, and the last stock was sold in 1925, ending all hope of a re-opening. The decision was taken by Watt's Belfast-dominated parent group, United Distillers, because of contraction in the market and the bane of the Derry economy throughout the 20th century: peripherality to external management. United Distillers opted to concentrate its Irish output in Belfast and had terminated all its Irish operations by 1929.[34]

The ITGWU motored on. In September 1921, it won a short recognition strike of red leaders in the shipyard, and in October it swapped its office in William Street for a 'hall', a former factory, at the corner of Richmond Street and Linenhall Street. The acquisition was celebrated with a lecture from O'Donnell on Labour and partition.[35] It encapsulated one of his life-long themes:

it is a mistake to assume that many Ulster workers are not in favour of Partition. They are. If anyone had got as many mobbings and howlings down in dealing with Ulster workers as he got they would have the same views. But this much he could say … He was certain that one could shake to pieces any Orange Lodge in Ulster where he was allowed to develop freely economic and national theories.[36]

He concluded by challenging James Turkington, founder of the Ulster Workers' Trade Union and recently in Derry, to a debate. The Derry branch had a full-time secretary, John F. Doherty, in 1922.[37]

DIVISION AND DECLINE

The picture was very different in 1923. O'Donnell had moved to Dublin. Ridgway had had to contend with other distractions, including an arrest in Monaghan by the RIC in 1922 and a jailbreak from Dundalk, and the ITGWU had abandoned its offices in Derry city. It was an annus horribilis for the OBU. Jim Larkin's egotistic clash with his executive split the union in June, and the long-awaited employers' 'big push' in July crushed the spirit of militancy in the Free State. The Derry branch had collapsed by October, leaving just two branches in Ulster, at Belfast and Old Engine.[38] The ASTT and the Tailors' and Garment Workers' Union soldiered on. The former had a part-time nursemaid in Sarah Doherty. The latter sent Annie Holmes to Derry in March 1923 as a full-time 'lady organizer to educate the women and girls'. Originally from Leeds, Miss Holmes was experienced in dealing with trade boards. When, on 2 April 1923, the shirtmaking trade board reduced wage rates to 7 per cent below British levels, accepting employer arguments that they needed to offset transport costs, serious poaching ensued.[39] The ASTT's Londonderry (Factory Workers) branch shrivelled to about 250 members after losing almost 3,000 women to the Tailors' and Garment Workers', which jumped from 403 to 3,308 members.[40] Shirt workers had crowded into the Guildhall in protest at the 7 per cent reduction and the trades council had pledged its backing. It was to little avail, and by 1926 the Derry membership of the Tailors' and Garment Workers' Union had fallen to 2,000. The ASTT branch had recovered a little, and grown to 810 members. It would soon dip into decline again. Relations between the two unions were downright nasty until adversity forced them to merge in 1932. Unity was further diluted by the defection of about half the cutters to the Amalgamated Transport and General Workers' Union. The beleaguered Miss Doherty complained repeatedly of poaching and the ASTT raised the issue with the British Trades Union Congress. The anomaly of a skilled elite joining a catch-all general union was usually attributed, by the cutters themselves, to the solidarity of the dockers during the 1920 strike, but the fear that belonging to a predominantly female union would facilitate the introduction of women to the job and lead to de-skilling is also likely to have been a factor. Excluding girls from the cutting rooms remained an abiding concern.[41]

The Amalgamated Transport and General Workers' Union had materialized in 1922 from one of the biggest mergers in British Labour history, and absorbed the NUDL among many others. This particular amalgamated was a *bête noire* of the ITGWU, which took it to court over the pirating of its distinctive title. Its general secretary, Ernest Bevin, the most powerful man in British trade unionism, spoke in Derry in March 1923 and deplored 'some of the literature and some of the stupid and foolish things done and said by the Irish Transport Union'. Unions, he said, should operate 'irrespective of frontiers and boundary lines'; an evasion that would become all too familiar to Irish Labour over the next 40 years.[42] In September, the Amalgamated Transport Union won a wage and recognition strike involving 100 vanmen and labourers in the bakery trade. It was one of 13 strikes that year, and one of three for a wage increase, and the following summer brought a clamour for the restoration of pay cuts.[43] But the industrial decline continued, with the shipyard suspending production. Once again, peripherality was the problem as Swan Hunter gave preference to their home yards.[44] For unemployed workers without employment insurance – and one needed a job in the first place to acquire insurance benefit – there was nothing to fall back on other than the possibility of temporary work on a relief scheme, charity or emigration. The unions' retreat was far from over. Since 1920, the trades council had featured annually in the *Derry almanac*. In 1924, its place was taken by the UULA, which was positioned, appropriately, beneath the Londonderry Employers' Federation.[45]

Conclusion

Jim Larkin made an obvious impact on Derry, positively in 1907–8 as an inspiration to trade union organization, and negatively in 1909 when the dockers decided to stick with the NUDL rather than go with the ITGWU. More generally, Derry produced a high-profile antagonist of Larkinism in James McCarron. If McCarron was not so much against Larkinite militancy as Larkin's republicanism and demand for an Irish-based trade unionism, he was nonetheless a rallying point for conservative elements in the ITUC. His successor as the foremost Derryman in Congress, Thomas Cassidy, blended into the Congress executive so smoothly as to be almost invisible to history, although he presided over the ITUC in momentous times.

The story of syndicalism in Derry was more complex. In some respects, Derry was as insulated from the south of Ireland as Belfast. Industrially it was tied more tightly to the war economy than southern cities. Its wartime trade unionism developed earlier and more steadily, from a stronger base, and was dominated by the amalgamateds. It is true that one British-based union, the NUR, was the leading advocate of industrial unionism, and of direct action to tackle the food supply crisis, in 1916–17, but by mid-1917 it was being overtaken by the far more radical ITGWU. Led by Peadar O'Donnell, the OBU became the cutting edge of social revolutionism in Derry, and for O'Donnell that meant linkage with the national revolution too. Derry trades council's phalanx against the ITGWU was unique, and would not have happened without the amalgamateds. At the same time, the trades council incrementally abandoned its implicit Redmondism for the more republican policies of the ITUC, and took its cue from Dublin, even on things as controversial in Ulster as conscription, the political prisoners strike, and the railway munitions strike. If Derry had none of the more swaggering expressions of Irish syndicalism – there were no soviets, no factory occupations, no radical newspapers, no Labour Party, no speeches from the trades council promising a Workers' Republic or a co-operative commonwealth, and no triumphalist 'red flaggery' – it did echo the zeitgeist with sympathetic action and efforts at promoting a working-class counter-culture through co-operatives, May Day concerts and sports days.

The First World War's most significant long-term consequence for Derry Labour was the unionization of women in the shirt factories. The process was underway before the war with the introduction of a trade board, and the second key factor was the establishment of a formal comparator with cross-channel age rates and then the creation of a differential with Britain. The huge expansion of union membership challenges assumptions about the weakness of pre-war trade unionism in the sector being due to gender. Men wanted women to organize, not necessarily in the same union if they were cutters, but that had more to do with protecting craft privilege rather than gender. And women would have organized had they had sufficient incentive and opportunity to surmount employer disapproval. This is not to say that gender was not an inhibitor, merely that it was not crucial.

Similar points can be made about sectarianism. The remarkable thing about trade unionism in Ulster is not how much but how little it was influenced by sectarianism. Ulster had a fractured society, tormented by religion and politics, with a layered hierarchy of references: provincial, Irish, British and imperial. These diversities were pressed together into a single economy with, for the most part, mixed workforces. They were also pushed into a single, anglo-centric trade unionism, Irish unions being generally too weak to compete before the birth of the ITGWU, and Unionism being too conservative an ideology to produce a Labour movement of worth: initiatives like the UULA merely highlighted the fact. People coped with the density of difference by compartmentalizing their mentalities and adjusting the response code in each. That learned behaviour made it easier to detach the trade unions from sectarianism, though the separation could never be complete. In a society in which religion mattered ubiquitously, including in the workplaces and the unions themselves, sectarianism inevitably curbed solidarity. And *parri passu*, the compartmentalization made unions more detached from politics, and ensured that militancy was less likely to mature into radicalism in the north than in the south or in Britain. It was enough for unions that Catholics and Protestants could unite on wages and conditions. There was a surreal example in the cutters' strike in 1920, carrying on regardless through the city's civil war, with the overwhelmingly nationalist dockers blacking 'tainted goods' in solidarity with the largely Protestant cutters. One could cite many other instances, and cases where behaviour was determined simply by an instinct for survival. Protestants on the Londonderry and Lough Swilly Railway stood united with colleagues dismissed during the railway munitions strike. Catholics on the Great Northern Railway showed their solidarity with their fellow workers by not joining the protest. With one economy and so many mixed workforces, such solidarity was not only the norm, it was an operational necessity.

The ITGWU's Derry campaign suggests that those in the Connolly tradition were not so naïve about the Protestant working class.[1] Cathal O'Shannon recognized that Unionists could combine conservative politics with wage militancy. O'Donnell warned against the delusion that Protestant workers did not want partition. Charlie Ridgway was a Belfast Protestant, convinced, as they all were, that Unionists could be won to the republic through socialism. Were it just a matter of choosing between the UULA and the ITGWU their faith might well have been vindicated. But, like a deus ex machina, the amalgamated resolved the dilemma by offering Unionists a form of trade unionism that was willing to be wage militant and just as willing to sideline the peculiarities of the Ulster question. The result was a brittle unity across the confessional divide at the expense of sugar-coating sectarianism with a veneer of class rhetoric, a trade unionism policed by a self-selecting oligarchy of officials, a provincial movement whose highest objective was to track cross-channel wage levels, and a dysfunctional Labour politics unable to gain a lasting traction. In Derry, that was enough for most nationalists too. However much the city did not want to be in Northern Ireland, its mindset was shaped by the British state.

Finally, in so far as the labour unrest of these years is remembered in Derry, it is recalled negatively. Strikes have been blamed for the end of the tramway, the distilleries, the coaling for the Great Northern Railway, and the decline of the shirt-factories. The perception is an old one, and a chronic problem for Labour in any provincial centre: capital cities have a way of looking after themselves. Writing in 1926, Annie Holmes complained of the 'fixed idea in the minds of the people in Derry city, many of whom are in a position to know that such a view can only have emanated from the employers' propaganda'.[2] In reality, the bane of the city was, and is, something its political leaders have never tackled: peripherality.

Appendix 1: Strikes in Derry city, 1907–23

(note that small strikes in Ireland often went unnoticed by the recording clerks)

No. of firms involved (where stated)	Strikers and workers affected	Numbers involved Directly-*indirectly*	Began	Ended	Issue (a wage increase, except where stated)
1907					
	Tailors	11–	Not given		Replacement of workers
	Dockers	40–	17 May	18 May	Wage cut
	Button-holers, etc.	17–*192*	6 Dec.	13 Dec.	Wage cut
1908					
1	Shirt and collar workers	1,023–	12 Sept.	17 Sept.	Wage cut
1909					
6	Carters	132–	1 Apr.	6 Apr.	
1910–11 no disputes recorded					
1912					
	Labourers	70–	31 Jan.	3 Feb.	Personnel issue
2	Bakers	30–	31 Dec.	Jan. 1913	
1913					
	Shirt and collar workers	1,200–	20 Feb.	12 Mar.	Wage cut
	Labourers, masons	17–*12*	24 July	26 July	
9	Carpenters, brick and stone layers, labourers	200–*100*	5 Aug.	3 Oct.	
	Platers' helpers	70–	13 Mar.	14 Mar.	Dismissal
	Ships' carpenters	13	21 Feb.	22 Feb.	
	Labourers	120	12 May	17 May	

No. of firms involved (where stated)	Strikers and workers affected	Numbers involved Directly-*indirectly*	Began	Ended	Issue (a wage increase, except where stated)
1914					
7	Carters	140–	4 Feb.	9 Feb.	
	Labourers, rivetters, platers, holders-on	220–*122*	27 Apr.	13 May	
	Shipyardmen	600–	1 Oct.	3 Oct.	For the removal of a yard policeman
	Rivetters, holders-on, heater boys	29–	18 Dec.	7 Jan. 1915	Calculation of wages
1915					
	Fitters	4–	25 Feb.	29 Mar.	
	Apprentices	60–	25 May	27 May	
	Fitters, blacksmiths, helpers	10–	12 July	26 July	
	Quay labourers	92–	25 Sept.	18 Oct.	
	Apprentice fitters	12–	14 Oct.	15 Oct.	
	Collar workers	160	25 Nov.	7 Dec.	For the removal of a forewoman
1916					
	Shirt and collar workers	18–	8 Mar.	20 Mar.	Refusal to work with women in cutting rooms
2	Dockers	100–	4 May	4 May	
	Bleachers	59–	27 June	22 July	Union recognition
	Milesmen, gangers	33–	3 July	21 Oct.	
	Apprentice fitters	11–	13 July	19 July	Personnel issue
	Apprentice platers, etc.	27–	24 July	4 Aug	Wage cut
7	Carters	200–	15 Sept.	20 Sept.	
	Builders' labourers	28–	2 Nov.	4 Nov.	

No. of firms involved (where stated)	Strikers and workers affected	Numbers involved Directly-*indirectly*	Began	Ended	Issue (a wage increase, except where stated)
1917					
4	Fitters, turners	100–	7 Apr.	13 Apr.	
1	Builders' labourers	59–	29 May	13 June	Dismissal
General	Bootmakers, repairers	50–	16 June	29 June	
6	Builders' labourers	130–	26 July	16 Aug.	
1	Platers, helpers, labourers	200–	12 Sept.	13 Sept.	Staff cuts
1	Local authority labourers	14–	12 Sept.	14 Sept.	
4	Engineers	80–	27 Nov.	28 Nov.	
1918					
42	Platers' helpers, labourers	42–*62*	1 Jan.	5 Jan.	
1	Platers, rivetters	127–*100*	14 Jan.	19 Jan.	
1	Packers, washers	14–*73*	25 Jan.	4 Feb.	
1	Drapery assistants	21–	18 Feb.	7 Mar.	
1	Cornmill workers	40–	25 Feb.	2 Mar.	
	Building workers	60–	6 May	10 May	
9	Carters, dockers	400–	23 May	25 May	
1	Hosiery workers	42–*158*	3 June	8 June	
1	Carpenters/joiners, labourers	80–*31*	7 June	12 June	
1	Heater boys	70–*300*	17 June	19 June	Conditions
5	Biscuit packers	135–*15*	24 June	29 June	
1	Rivetters, platers, caulkers	350–	27 June	1 July	
1	Bottlers, storemen, vanmen	73–	2 Aug.	10 Aug.	
1	Blacksmiths	16–	6 Aug.	12 Aug.	
14	Tailors	125–	11 Nov.	3 Dec.	
3	Pork curers	76–	13 Dec.	14 Jan. 1919	

No. of firms involved (where stated)	Strikers and workers affected	Numbers involved Directly-*indirectly*	Began	Ended	Issue (a wage increase, except where stated)
1919					
1	Conductors, drivers, stablemen, foremen	10–2	18 Jan.	5 Feb.	
1	Platers, etc.	136–*273*	28 Jan.	1 Mar.	Wage cut
10	Painters	17–	1 Mar.	3 Mar.	
1	[public authority] drivers, collectors	21–	3 Mar.	8 Mar.	Dismissal
1	Mineral water bottle washers	16–	10 Mar.	15 Mar.	Dismissal
1	Building craftsmen, labourers	99–	8 May	17 July	
1	Cabinetmakers, upholsterers, french polishers	17–	8 May	30 May	
1	Caulkers, rivetters	250–	9 May	3 June	Wage cut
1	Plumbers, helpers	33–*12*	10 May	June	
	Labourers, shunters, etc.	29–	19 May	30 May	
3	Carpenters/joiners	21–	1 July	1 July	
13	Bottlers, vanmen, mineral water operatives	70–	10 July	6 Aug.	
1	Sawyers, labourers	13–	27 Aug.	4 Oct.	
1	Ship painters	23–	10 Sept.	8 Oct.	
6	Bakers	130–	27 Sept.	29 Sept.	
1	Seed merchant labourers	18–	6 Oct.	30 Oct.	
	Compositors, linotype operatives, bookbinders	66–*6*	20 Nov.	24 Nov.	
1920					
1	Foundry labourers	15–	No further details		

No. of firms involved (where stated)	Strikers and workers affected	Numbers involved Directly-*indirectly*	Began	Ended	Issue (a wage increase, except where stated)
1	Heater boys	40–	1 Mar.	2 Mar.	Replacement of workers
	Tailors	50	19 Apr.	Not given	
	Bakers	150–	3 May	17 May	
8	Builders' labourers	150–	10 May	15 May	
	Printers	4–	9 June	19 July	
Derry, Belfast, etc.	Shirt collar cutters	312–*17,000*	12 June	21 Aug.	
	Dockers, carters, yardmen, etc.	400–*100*	14 June	18 June	
1	Plumbers, labourers	33–*20*	10 Sept.	16 Sept.	
3	Electricians	30–	25 Sept.	10 Nov.	
3 in Belfast and Derry	Distillery workers	600–	23 Nov.	25 Nov.	
1921					
	Dockers	100–	23 Apr.	28 Apr.	Conditions
	Joiners	50–	6 May	22 July	Wage cut
	Distillers	150	7 June	22 July	Wage cut
	Red leaders (shipbuilding)	28–	14 Sept.	24 Sept.	Victimization
	Carters	350–	26 Sept.	27 Sept.	Wage cut
1922					
	Harbour employees	31–*1*	13 Jan.	21 Jan.	Wage cut
1	Plumbers	21–	1 Feb.	14 Feb.	Personnel issue
	Dockers	60–	9 May	11 May	Personnel issue
1	Lough Swilly railwaymen	62–	28 May	1 June	Refusal to work with other workers

No. of firms involved (where stated)	Strikers and workers affected	Numbers involved Directly-*indirectly*	Began	Ended	Issue (a wage increase, except where stated)
12	Painters	100–	10 June	15 Aug.	Wage cut
	Dockers	57–	2 Sept.	9 Sept.	Dismissal
2	Plumbers, gasfitters	10–	7 Sept.	17 Sept.	Wage cut
	Dockers	150–	27 Sept.	28 Sept.	Conditions
	Carters	250–	28 Sept.	12 Oct.	Wage cut
1923					
1	Apprentice platers, shipwrights	149–	27 Jan.	19 Mar.	
12	Building craftsmen, labourers	200–50	1 May	10 May	Wage cut
1	Blacksmith, hammermen	14–	17 May	23 May	
12	Shirtmakers	12–	5 July	11 July	Wage cut
15	Fancy linen smoothers	15–	18 July	21 July	Wages
	Relief scheme labourers	30–	4 Aug.	16 Aug.	Wages
1	Clerks, station masters, etc.	60–*239*	6 Aug.	9 Aug.	Dismissal
	Harbour labourers	25–	13 Aug.	15 Aug.	Wage cut
	Carters	150–	15 Aug.	15 Aug.	Wage cut
6	Labourers, packers, vanmen	100–	22 Sept.	28 Sept.	
1	Clerks, station masters, etc.	60–*239*	24 Sept.	25 Sept.	Dismissal
	Busmen, cleaners	18–	23 Oct.	26 Oct.	Dismissal
	Dockers	106–	3 Dec.	6 Dec.	Dismissal

Source: TNA, Ministry of Labour records, LAB 34/7–20, LAB 34/25–39, LAB 34/40–41.

Appendix 2: Affiliations to Derry and District Trades and Labour Council, 1893 and 1920–3

Affiliates (by official name or as cited)	1893	1920	1921	1922	1923
Asylum Attendants, Derry		✓	✓	✓	✓
Asylum Attendants, Letterkenny		✓	✓	✓	✓
Automobile Union, Irish		✓	✓	✓	
Bakers, Irish Federated	✓				
Bakers' and Confectioners' Amalgamated Union, Irish			✓	✓	✓
Boilermakers		✓	✓	✓	✓
Boot and Shoemakers, Amalgamated	✓				
Boxmakers		✓	✓	✓	✓
Brick and Stonelayers, Ancient Guild of Incorporated	✓				
Butchers		✓	✓	✓	✓
Cabinetmakers, Amalgamated	✓				
Carpenters and Joiners, Amalgamated Society of	✓	✓	✓	✓	✓
Clerks, National Union of		✓	✓	✓	✓
Coachbuilders, Amalgamated	✓				
Coopers		✓	✓	✓	✓
Electrical Trades' Union		✓	✓	✓	✓
Engineers, Amalgamated Society of		✓	✓	✓	✓
Gasworkers and General Labourers, National Union of	✓				
Insurance Agents		✓	✓	✓	✓
Labour, Knights of	✓				
Labour, National Amalgamated Union of		✓	✓	✓	✓
Labourers, National Union of Dock		✓	✓	✓	✓

Union					
Locomotive Engineers and Firemen, Associated Society of		✓	✓	✓	✓
Masons and Bricklayers	✓	✓	✓	✓	✓
Municipal Employees' Association		✓	✓	✓	✓
Musicians' Union		✓	✓	✓	✓
Painters and Decorators		✓	✓	✓	✓
Plasterers' Union		✓	✓	✓	✓
Plumbers, United Operative		✓	✓	✓	✓
Postmen's Federation		✓	✓	✓	✓
Railway Clerks' Association		✓			
Railway Servants, Amalgamated Society of	✓				
Sailors and Firemen, National Amalgamated Union of	✓				
Sailors and Firemen, National Union of		✓	✓	✓	✓
Shipbuilders' Helpers' Association, Associated Scottish Iron	✓				
Shipping Clerks		✓	✓		
Shipwrights, Associated	✓				
Shirtcutters' Union		✓	✓	✓	✓
Stonemasons, Operative	✓				
Tailors		✓	✓	✓	✓
Tailors and Tailoresses, Amalgamated Society of	✓	✓	✓		
Teachers, Derry City and County		✓	✓	✓	✓
Teachers' Association, Donegal		✓	✓	✓	✓
Teachers' Association, Gweedore and Rosses		✓	✓	✓	✓
Woodcutters		✓	✓	✓	✓

Source: The Derry almanac, north-west directory, and general advertiser (Londonderry, 1893, 1920–3)

Notes

ASTT	Amalgamated Society of Tailors and Tailoresses
HC	House of Commons parliamentary papers
IRA	Irish Republican Army
ITGWU	Irish Transport and General Workers' Union
ITUC	Irish Trades Union Congress
NAUL	National Amalgamated Union of Labour
NLI	National Library of Ireland
NUDL	National Union of Dock Labourers
NUR	National Union of Railwaymen
OBU	One Big Union
ODNB	*Oxford dictionary of national biography*
QUB	Queen's University, Belfast
RIC	Royal Irish Constabulary
TNA	The National Archives, London
UGW	United Garment Workers' Union
UULA	Ulster Unionist Labour Association
UUMC	Ulster University, Magee College

INTRODUCTION

1 UUMC, *Report of the seventeenth Irish Trades Union Congress* (Dublin, 1910), p. 21. By 'Labour' is meant the organizations and activists of trade unions and related groups. Workers are otherwise referred to as 'labour'. To distinguish them from trade unionists, the convention is followed of citing supporters of the union with Britain as Unionists, whether members of the Unionist Party or not. The ITUC changed its name to the ITUC and Labour Party in 1914 and the Irish Labour Party and Trade Union Congress in 1918. To minimize confusion, it will be referred to as the ITUC or Congress throughout.

2 See Emmet O'Connor, 'Old wine in new bottles? Syndicalism and "fakirism" in the great labour unrest, 1911–1914', *Labour History Review*, 79:1 (2014), 19–36.

3 Cost of living of the working classes. *Report of an enquiry by the Board of Trade into working-class rents and retail prices,* together with the rates of wages in certain occupations in industrial towns of the United Kingdom in 1912 (in continuation of a similar enquiry in 1905), HC 1913 (Cd.6955), lxvi, pp 115, 117, 119, 123, 294.

4 For the shirt industry see Julie Ann Grew, 'The Derry shirt making industry, 1831–1913' (MPhil, University of Ulster, 1987), pp 208–14.

5 For Derry, the best of the biographies are Dónal Ó Drisceoil, *Peadar O'Donnell* (Cork, 2001); Peter Hegarty, *Peadar O'Donnell* (Cork, 1999); Anton McCabe, 'The stormy petrel of the transport workers: Peadar O'Donnell, trade unionist, 1917–20', *Saothar*, 19 (1994), 41–51; Michael McInerney, *Peadar O'Donnell: Irish social rebel* (Dublin, 1974), is virtually a memoir; O'Donnell's other relevant memoirs are *There will be another day* (Dublin, 1963); and *Not yet Emmet: a wreath on the grave of Sean Murray* (Dublin, 1985).

6 Andrew Robert Finlay, 'Trade unionism and sectarianism among Derry shirt

workers, 1920–1968, with special
reference to the National Union of
Tailors and Garment Workers' (PhD,
University College London, 1989); Alan
Robinson, 'A social geography of the
city of Londonderry' (MA, Queen's
University, Belfast, 1967).

7   Ronan Gallagher, *Violence and nationalist
politics in Derry city, 1920–1923* (Dublin,
2003); Brian Lacy, *Siege city: the story
of Derry and Londonderry* (Belfast,
1990); Desmond Murphy, *Derry,
Donegal, and modern Ulster, 1790–1921*
(Londonderry, 1981); Gerard O'Brien,
*Derry and Londonderry: history & society:
interdisciplinary essays on the history of an
Irish county* (Dublin, 1999); Robert Gavin,
William Kelly and Dolores O'Reilly,
*Atlantic gateway: the port and city of
Londonderry since 1700* (Dublin, 2009).

8   See 'The folly of Andrew Watt', *Derry
Journal*, 31 Oct. 2007.

I. LARKINISM, 1907–14

1   On Larkin, see C. Desmond Greaves,
'Jim Larkin's earliest years', *Irish
Democrat*, Sept. 1980; Donal Nevin,
'Early years in Liverpool' in Donal
Nevin (ed.), *James Larkin: lion of the fold*
(Dublin, 1998), pp 133–43; and Emmet
Larkin, *James Larkin: Irish labour leader,
1876–1947* (London, 1965), pp 3–22.

2   UUMC, *Report of the thirteenth Irish Trades
Union Congress*, Athlone (1906), pp 82–3;
*Report of the fourteenth Irish Trades Union
Congress* (Dublin, 1907), pp 59–60; John
Cunningham, *Labour in the west of Ireland:
working life and struggle, 1890–1914* (Belfast,
1995), pp 65–71.

3   *Derry Journal*, 27 Mar. 1907; Board of
Trade (Labour Department), *Report
on trade unions in 1905–1907*, HC 1909
(Cd.4651), lxxxix, p. 132.

4   Peter Gerard Collins, 'Belfast trades
council, 1881–1921' (PhD, Queen's
University, Belfast, 1988), appendix 3;
Malcolm Wallace, 'Single or return?
the official history of the Transport
Salaried Staffs' Association', available at
http:www.tssa.org.uk/about/single-or-
return/chapter05.htm, accessed 17 May
2015; *Derry Journal*, 7, 30 Nov. 1906, 8
Mar., 8 May 1907; Grew, 'The Derry
shirt making industry, 1831–1913', p. 223.

5   *Derry Journal*, 8 Mar., 27 Apr., 8, 18 May,
5 July 1907.

6   UUMC, *Report of the twenty-second Irish
Trades Union Congress and Labour Party*
(Sligo, 1916), p. 19.

7   UUMC, *Report of the seventeenth Irish Trades
Union Congress* (Dundalk, 1910), pp 11–12.

8   UUMC, *Report of the fourteenth Irish Trades
Union Congress*, pp 17–21; *Report of the
seventeenth Irish Trades Union Congress*, p. 61.

9   *Derry Journal*, 20–4 May 1907.

10 Finlay, 'Trade unionism and sectarianism
among Derry shirt workers, 1920–1968',
p. 355.

11 *Derry Journal*, 8 Mar. 1907; Cunningham,
Labour in the west of Ireland, p. 62.

12 The National Archives, London (TNA),
Ministry of Labour reports on strikes
and lockouts, LAB 34/7 to 34/32.

13 John Gray, *City in revolt: James Larkin and
the Belfast dock strike of 1907* (Belfast, 1985),
p. 226, fn. 15.

14 *Derry Journal*, 8 July 1907.

15 The family tradition is insistent on
his Ulster nativity, despite academic
scepticism. See Jim Larkin, *In the footsteps
of Big Jim: a family biography* (Dublin,
1995), pp 3–9.

16 *Derry Journal*, 8 July 1907.

17 *Derry Journal*, 24–9 July.

18 How long the Textile Operatives'
Association survived is unclear. It
was not listed among affiliates of the
National Federation of Women Workers
in annual reports of the Women's Trade
Union League in 1907, 1908 or 1910.
Finlay, 'Trade unionism and sectarianism
among Derry shirt workers, 1920–1968',
p. 88; *Derry Journal*, 8 Nov. 1907.

19 *Derry Journal*, 23 Aug. 1907; *Londonderry
Sentinel*, 27 Aug. 1907.

20 *Derry Journal*, 11–18 Sept. 1907.

21 *Derry Journal*, 8–22 Nov. 1907; *Derry
Standard*, 15 Nov. 1907; *Londonderry
Sentinel*, 16–21 Nov. 1907.

22 *Derry Journal*, 11, 18–20 Dec. 1907; TNA,
Ministry of Labour reports on strikes
and lockouts, LAB 34/25.

23 *Derry Journal*, 18 Oct. 1907.

24 *Derry Journal*, 25 May, 17 May 1908;
TNA, Ministry of Labour reports on
strikes and lockouts, LAB 34/26.

25 Gray, *City in revolt*, p. 192; Dermot
Keogh, *The rise of the Irish working class:*

the Dublin trade union movement and Labour
leadership, 1890–1914 (Belfast, 1982), p 133.

26 C. Desmond Greaves, *The Irish transport
and general workers' union: the formative
years, 1909–23* (Dublin, 1982), p. 25.

27 Larkin, *James Larkin*, p. 70; Greaves, *The
Irish Transport and General Workers' Union*,
p. 29.

28 William Kenefick, 'James O'Connor
Kessack', *Oxford dictionary of national
biography*, online; *Irish Worker*, 3 June 1911.

29 Gray, *City in revolt*, pp 198–203; and
Greaves, *The Irish Transport and General
Workers' Union*, pp 29–31.

30 *Derry Journal*, 15 Jan. 1909.

31 On the Belfast debacle, see Gray, *City in
revolt*, pp 198–203; and Greaves, *The Irish
Transport and General Workers' Union*, pp
29–31.

32 Thomas J. Morrissey, SJ, *William
O'Brien, 1881–1968: socialist, republican,
Dáil Deputy, editor and trade union leader*
(Dublin, 2007); UUMC, *Report of the
sixteenth Irish Trades Union Congress*
(Limerick, 1909), pp 15–16, 40–2, 48;
Irish Labour Journal, 19 June 1909.

33 UUMC, *Report of the seventeenth Irish
Trades Union Congress*, pp 11–12.

34 UUMC, *Report of the seventeenth Irish
Trades Union Congress*, pp 23–5.

35 UUMC, *Report of the sixteenth Irish
Trades Union Congress*, p. 50; *Report of the
seventeenth Irish Trades Union Congress*, pp
25–30, 61.

36 *Harp*, June 1910.

37 Donal Nevin (ed.), *Between comrades:
James Connolly, letters and correspondence,
1889–1916* (Dublin, 2007), pp 427–8.

38 UUMC, *Report of the nineteenth Irish
Trades Union Congress* (Clonmel, 1912), pp
61, 69–70, 77–9.

39 UUMC, *William O'Brien papers*,
13908(iii).

40 *Irish Worker*, 17, 31 May 1913.

41 UUMC, *Report of the twentieth Irish Trades
Union Congress*, Cork (1913), pp 35–6;
Nevin (ed.), *Between comrades*, p. 491.

42 UUMC, *Report of the twentieth Irish Trades
Union Congress*, p. 66.

43 Cited in Nevin (ed.), *James Larkin*, p. 467.

44 The telegram implies some uncertainty
about the date, as the *Furnissia* was due
on 25 July but Connolly cabled on 26
July. See Nevin, *James Connolly*, p. 379;

Nevin (ed.), *Between comrades*, p. 426; C.
Desmond Greaves, *The life and times of
James Connolly* (London, 1961), p. 201;
Samuel Levenson, *James Connolly: a
biography* (London, 1977), pp 178, 180.

45 Nora Connolly O'Brien, *Portrait of a rebel
father* (Dublin, 1935), pp 110–15.

46 *Derry Journal*, 21 Aug., 11 Sept. 1911.

47 *Derry Journal*, 25–7 Sept. 1911.

48 TNA, Ministry of Labour reports on
strikes and lockouts, LAB 34/10 to 34/39.

49 *Derry Journal*, 15 Aug. 1913.

50 Greaves, *The Irish Transport and General
Workers' Union*, p. 116.

51 *Derry Journal*, 26–8 Nov. 1913.

52 *Irish Worker*, 25 May 1911.

53 *Londonderry Sentinel*, 9 Sept. 1913; *Derry
Journal*, 6 June 1919.

54 *Derry Journal*, 30 Jan.–11 Feb., 28–30
Mar., 8 Apr. 1914; TNA, Ministry of
Labour reports on strikes and lockouts,
LAB 34/32. Despite the name change,
the union continued to be known as
the NUDL. In Derry it sometimes
advertised itself as the 'NUDL and
Riverside Workers and Carters'. See
Derry Journal, 28 Apr. 1919.

55 Brendan Mark Browne, 'Trade boards
in Northern Ireland, 1909–45' (PhD,
Queen's University, Belfast, 1989), pp
45–108.

56 Finlay, 'Trade unionism and sectarianism
among Derry shirt workers, 1920–1968',
pp 71, 74, 87–8, 355.

57 Gavin, Kelly and O'Reilly, *Atlantic
gateway*, p. 170.

58 *Derry Journal*, 29 June 1914.

59 UUMC, *Report of the twenty first Irish Trades
Union Congress*, Dublin (1914), p. 104.

60 Ibid., pp 66–7, 94.

61 Emmet O'Connor, *A labour history of
Waterford* (Waterford, 1989), p. 130.

2. BOOM, 1914–20

1 Henry Pelling, *A history of British trade
unionism* (London, 1971), pp 149–51.

2 *Working classes cost of living committee,
report*, HC 1918 (Cd.8980), vii, p. 831.
The committee considered evidence in
Britain only.

3 UUMC, *Report of the twenty-third Irish
Trades Union Congress and Labour Party*,
Derry (1917), pp 25–8.

4 Donal Nevin (ed.), *Trade union century*
(Dublin, 1994), p. 433.

5   Gavin, Kelly and O'Reilly, *Atlantic gateway*, pp 179, 205.

6   Captain J.R. White, DSO, *Misfit: an autobiography* (London, 1930), p. 307.

7   See Colm Fox, *The making of a minority: political developments in Derry and the north, 1912–25* (Derry, 1997).

8   *Derry Journal*, 8 July 1918.

9   Richard Doherty, 'Derry and the First World War' in *From home to foreign fields: a history of the First World War in the Derry City, Strabane District, Omagh District and Donegal County Council areas* (Peace III, n.d.), pp 15–16. Accurate tallies are impossible, as strangers enlisted in Derry, and some locals enlisted elsewhere.

10   Thomas P. Dooley, *Irishmen or English soldiers? The times and world of a southern Catholic Irish man (1876–1916) enlisting in the British army during the First World War* (Liverpool, 1995), pp 4–8, 124–5.

11   *Derry Journal*, 6 June 1919.

12   *Derry Journal*, 21 July, 6 Aug. 1919.

13   *Derry Journal*, 10 Feb. 1915.

14   UUMC, *Report of the twenty-second Irish Trades Union Congress*, p. 19.

15   Chamber of Commerce, annual general meeting, *Derry Journal*, 25 Feb. 1918.

16   *Derry Journal*, 4 Mar. 1918.

17   Noel Browne, *Against the tide* (Dublin, 1986), pp 1–2.

18   *Derry Journal*, 22, 27 Feb. 1918.

19   Mary Ida Milne, 'The 1918–19 influenza pandemic in Ireland: a Leinster perspective' (PhD, Trinity College Dublin, 2010), p. 248.

20   Browne, 'Trade boards in Northern Ireland, 1909–45', pp 146–62, 340.

21   *Derry Journal*, 8 June 1914, 30 Apr., 26 May 1915, 10 Mar. 1916; Finlay, 'Trade unionism and sectarianism among Derry shirt workers, 1920–1968', pp 71, 74, 87–8, 355; TNA, Ministry of Labour reports on strikes and lockouts, LAB 34/33–34.

22   Gavin, Kelly and O'Reilly, *Atlantic gateway*, pp 170–1, 185–6; *Derry Journal*, 17, 20 May 1920.

23   *Derry Journal*, 21 Feb., 19 May 1919.

24   Gavin, Kelly and O'Reilly, *Atlantic gateway*, p. 171.

25   *Derry Journal*, 6 May 1918.

26   *Derry Journal*, 7 May 1915.

27   TNA, RIC inspectors' monthly reports, Feb. 1920, CO 904/111.

28   *Derry Journal*, 18 July 1917.

29   McCabe, 'The stormy petrel of the transport workers', 47.

30   TNA, RIC intelligence reports, 1918, CO 904/19/3–5.

31   *Derry Journal*, 14 Jan. 1916, 2 Apr., 3–27 Aug. 1917, 9–23 Aug. 1918, 28 Apr., 9 July 1919; TNA, Ministry of Labour reports on strikes and lockouts, LAB34/37; RIC inspectors' reports, Apr.–May 1919, CO 904/108–109; Donnan Harvey, 'Labour in Donegal, 1917–23' (MA, University of Ulster, 2006); *Voice of Labour*, 17 Aug. 1918.

32   Eric Taplin, *The Dockers' Union: a study of the National Union of Dock Labourers, 1889–1922* (Leicester, 1985), pp 125, 130–1; TNA, Ministry of Labour reports on strikes and lockouts, LAB 34/33–36.

33   *New Way*, Sep., Dec. 1917; Conor McCabe, 'The Amalgamated Society of Railway Servants and the National Union of Railwaymen in Ireland, 1911–1923' (PhD, University of Ulster, 2006), p. 84.

34   UUMC, *Report of the twenty-third Irish Trades Union Congress and Labour Party*, p. 59; *Report of the twenty-fifth Irish Labour Party and Trade Union Congress*, Drogheda (1919), p. 147.

35   *Derry Journal*, 5 June 1916, 14 May, 9 July, 10 Sep. 1917, 10 June 1918; *Voice of Labour*, 8 Dec. 1917.

36   *Derry Journal*, 27 Feb. 1918.

37   Gavin, Kelly and O'Reilly, *Atlantic gateway*, p. 182; *Derry Journal*, 5 Nov. 1917, 22 Dec. 1919, 14 Apr., 8 May 1920; McCabe, 'The stormy petrel of the transport workers', 47.

38   UUMC, *Report of the twenty-sixth Irish Labour Party and Trade Union Congress*, Cork (1920), p. 159.

39   The totals for strikers and strike-days exclude a strike of distillery operatives in Derry and Belfast, and the shirt cutters' strike, mainly in Derry but also in other centres, for which no separate Derry figures are available.

40   *Derry Journal*, 29 Jan., 6 June 1919.

41   *Derry Journal*, 31 Mar. 1919.

42   *Derry Journal*, 4 Apr. 1919.

43   *Derry Journal*, 3 Feb. 1919; *Voice of Labour*, 8 Feb., 8 March, 5 Apr., 14 June 1919; Austen Morgan, *Labour and partition: the*

Belfast working class, 1905–23 (London, 1991), pp 243–4; TNA, RIC Inspectors General's monthly confidential reports, 1 Jan.–30 Apr. 1919, CO 904/108.

44 UUMC, *Report of the twenty-second Irish Trades Union Congress*, pp 40, 67, 76; Census, 1911.

45 *Derry Journal*, 14 May 1917.

46 UUMC, *Report of the twenty-third Irish Trades Union Congress and Labour Party*, pp 13, 22–3, 40–8, 55–8, 75, 89–92; *Derry Journal*, 10 Aug. 1917, 24 Jan. 1919.

47 UUMC, *Report of the twenty-third Irish Trades Union Congress and Labour Party*, pp 51–3.

48 *Derry Journal*, 22 Apr. 1918; *Londonderry Sentinel*, 23 Apr. 1918; *New Way*, May 1918.

49 *Derry Journal*, 22 Apr., 10 June 1918; O'Donnell, *There will be another day*, p. 16.

50 UUMC, *Report of the twenty-fourth Irish Labour Party and Trade Union Congress and of the special congress*, Waterford (1918), pp 14–15.

51 Morgan, *Labour and partition*, pp 193–4.

52 UUMC, *Report of the twenty-fourth Irish Labour Party and Trade Union Congress and of the special congress*, p. 6.

53 *Derry Journal*, 14–18 Oct. 1918, 8 Mar. 1920.

54 *Derry Journal*, 14 Feb. 1919, 23 May 1921; TNA, RIC inspectors' monthly reports, Feb. 1919, CO 904/108; *Coleraine Chronicle*, 14 May 1921.

55 Lacy, *Siege city*, pp 223–4; *Derry Journal*, 28 Apr.–2 May 1919; Liam Cahill, *Forgotten revolution: Limerick soviet 1919, a threat to British power in Ireland* (Dublin, 1990), p. 130.

56 *Derry Journal*, 9–11 Dec. 1918; T.J. O'Connell, *100 years of progress: the story of the Irish National teachers' Organisation, 1868–1968* (Dublin, 1968), p. 29; John Cunningham, *Unlikely radicals: Irish post-primary teachers and the ASTI, 1909–2009* (Cork, 2009), pp 46–7.

57 Emmet O'Connor, *Syndicalism in Ireland, 1917–23* (Cork, 1988), pp 178–9.

58 *Derry Journal*, 12 Nov. 1919

59 *Londonderry Sentinel*, 13 Apr. 1920.

60 *Derry Journal*, 7, 21, Jan., 2 Feb. 1920, 21 Feb. 1923; *Watchword of Labour*, 31 Jan. 1920; Ronan Gallagher, *Violence and nationalist politics in Derry city, 1920–23* (Dublin, 2003), p. 67.

61 *Londonderry Sentinel*, 15 Apr. 1920.

62 *Derry Journal*, 14–16 Apr., 26 May 1920.

63 *Derry Journal*, 28 July 1920.

64 *Londonderry Sentinel*, 10–13, 22 July 1920.

65 Arthur Mitchell, *Labour in Irish politics, 1890–1930: the Irish labour movement in an age of revolution* (Dublin, 1974), pp 120–2.

66 *Voice of Labour*, 31 Aug., 7 Sep. 1918.

3. SLUMP, 1920–3

1 *Annual report of the Ministry of Labour for Northern Ireland for the year 1922* (Belfast, 1922), p. 18; *Report of the Ministry of Labour for Northern Ireland for the years 1923–24* (Belfast, 1924), pp 34–5; Paul Edward Starrett, 'The Irish Transport and General Workers' Union in its industrial and political context, 1909–1923' (PhD, University of Ulster, 1986), p. 262; O'Connor, *Syndicalism in Ireland, 1917–23*, p. 98.

2 *Derry Journal*, 16 Apr. 1920; Gallagher, *Violence and nationalist politics in Derry city, 1920–23*, pp 20–42; Lacy, *Siege city*, pp 228–9; *Derry Journal*, 19 Apr. 1920; *Londonderry Sentinel*, 20 July 1920.

3 National Archives of Ireland, Belfast boycott (Mar. 1921), DE 2/110; Belfast: Atrocities on Catholics, 1920–21, DE 2/353.

4 *Derry Journal*, 20 Apr. 1921.

5 O'Connor, *Syndicalism in Ireland*, pp 98–102; National Library of Ireland (NLI), ITGWU *Annual report*, 1922, p. 6.

6 *Derry Journal*, 6 Oct. 1920, 24 Jan. 1921.

7 Browne, 'Trade boards in Northern Ireland, 1909–45', pp 221–66.

8 *Derry Journal*, 1 Jan. 1923.

9 Gavin, Kelly and O'Reilly, *Atlantic gateway*, p. 205.

10 NLI, ITGWU, *Annual Report for 1919*, 13318i4; Hegarty, *Peadar O'Donnell*, pp 64–5.

11 *Derry Journal*, 10–12 Feb. 1920.

12 *Watchword of Labour*, 28 Feb. 1920; *Derry Journal*, 20 Sept. 1920.

13 *Derry Journal*, 19 Nov. 1920; McCabe, 'The stormy petrel of the Transport Workers', 49.

14 McCabe, 'The stormy petrel of the Transport Workers', 47.

15 Ó Drisceoil, *Peadar O'Donnell*, pp 16–17; Hegarty, *Peadar O'Donnell*, pp 64–80; Gavin, Kelly and O'Reilly,

Atlantic gateway, p. 187; Starrett, 'The Irish Transport and General Workers' Union in its industrial and political context, 1909–1923', p. 332; Finlay, 'Trade unionism and sectarianism among Derry shirt workers, 1920–1968', p. 122; McCabe, 'The stormy petrel of the Transport Workers', 47; Colm Fox, *The making of a minority; political developments in Derry and the north, 1912–25* (Derry, 1997).

16 O'Donnell, *Not yet Emmet*, p. 9.

17 Hegarty, *Peadar O'Donnell*, p. 67.

18 TNA, RIC, Crime Department, Special Branch, strikes engineered by the ITGW Union, Feb. 1920 to Oct. 1921, CO 904/158.

19 *Londonderry Sentinel*, 31 July, 19 Aug. 1920; Finlay, 'Trade unionism and sectarianism among Derry shirt workers', pp 109–10, 113, 119; *Derry Journal*, 9 Apr. 1923.

20 As recalled by a cutter in Finlay, 'Trade unionism and sectarianism among Derry shirt workers', p. 106.

21 *Watchword of Labour*, 31 July, 21 Aug. 1920; Francis Devine, *Organizing history: a centenary of SIPTU, 1909–2009* (Dublin, 2009), p. 905.

22 In 1921, the ITGWU issued the first Irish edition of Connolly's *The axe to the root and old wine in new bottles*. *The axe to the root* was published in the United States in 1908. *Old wine in new bottles* was added from articles written by Connolly for *Forward* and *New Age* in April and May 1914.

23 Finlay, 'Trade unionism and sectarianism among Derry shirt workers', p. 108; *Derry Journal*, 6, 11, 13, 27 Aug., 3 Sep. 1920; *Watchword of Labour*, 4–11 Sept. 1920; *Londonderry Sentinel*, 5, 17–21 Aug. 190.

24 McInerney, *Peadar O'Donnell*, p. 39.

25 Ó Drisceoil, *Peadar O'Donnell*, pp 14–16, 101; McCabe, 'The stormy petrel of the Transport Workers', 48.

26 *Derry Journal*, 18 Apr., 27 May, 24 June, 9, 30 Sept. 1921.

27 *Derry Journal*, 5, 12, 19 Aug. 1921; *Derry Standard*, 12 Aug. 1921.

28 *Derry Journal*, 22 June, 10 Oct. 1921.

29 Finlay, 'Trade unionism and sectarianism among Derry shirt workers', p. 122.

30 *Derry Journal*, 19 Nov. 1921.

31 *Derry Journal*, 6 June, 27 July 1921; Finlay, 'Trade unionism and sectarianism among Derry shirt workers', p. 122.

32 *Derry Journal*, 17 June 1921.

33 *Derry Journal*, 18, 27 July 1921.

34 Gavin, Kelly and O'Reilly, *Atlantic gateway*, pp 186–9.

35 *Derry Journal*, 26–8 Sept., 3, 14 Oct., 18 Nov. 1921.

36 *Derry Journal*, 18 Nov. 1921.

37 NLI, ITGWU. Conference of organisers and full-time branch secretaries, correspondence and papers, Mar.–Apr. 1922.

38 UUMC, *Report of the twenty-eighth Irish Labour Party and Trade Union Congress*, Dublin (1922), pp 145–6; *Derry Journal*, 2 Mar. 1923; NLI, ITGWU, correspondence re delegate conference, Oct. 1923, 27065(1).

39 *Derry Journal*, 2 Mar. 1923, 7 Mar. 1924; Finlay, 'Trade unionism and sectarianism among Derry shirt workers', p. 356; Gavin, Kelly and O'Reilly, *Atlantic gateway*, p. 192.

40 *Derry Journal*, 7 Mar. 1924.

41 Finlay, 'Trade unionism and sectarianism among Derry shirt workers', pp 126–33, 195–9, 220–2, 356.

42 *Derry Journal*, 30 Mar. 1923.

43 TNA, Ministry of Labour records, LAB 34/41; *Derry Journal*, May–June 1924.

44 Gavin, Kelly and O'Reilly, *Atlantic gateway*, pp 175–8.

45 *The Derry almanac, north-west directory, and general advertiser* (Londonderry, 1924), p. 86.

CONCLUSION

1 Finlay, 'Trade unionism and sectarianism among Derry shirt workers, 1920–1968', is concerned chiefly with debunking what he presents as the Connolly tradition's analysis of northern Labour.

2 Quoted in Finlay, 'Trade unionism and sectarianism among Derry shirt workers', p. 197; see also Robinson, 'A social geography of the city of Londonderry', p. 109.